# BET

## LEADING AND SUCCEEDING

# ON

## IN BUSINESS AND IN LIFE

# ME

## ANNETTE VERSCHUREN
## WITH ELEANOR BEATON

HARPERCOLLINS PUBLISHERS LTD

*Bet On Me*
Copyright © 2016 by Annette Verschuren
Foreword © 2016 by David Johnston
All rights reserved.

Published by HarperCollins Publishers Ltd

First published by HarperCollins Publishers Ltd in a hardcover edition: 2016
This trade paperback edition: 2017

HarperCollins books may be purchased for educational, business, or sales
promotional use through our Special Markets Department.

HarperCollins Publishers Ltd
2 Bloor Street East, 20th Floor
Toronto, Ontario, Canada  M4W 1A8

*www.harpercollins.ca*

Library and Archives Canada Cataloguing in Publication
information is available upon request.

ISBN 978-1-44343-760-8

Printed and bound in the United States of America
LSC/H 9 8 7 6 5 4 3 2 1

*This book is for my family:*
*Tony and Annie Verschuren, Dorothy Tennant,*
*Turk, Andy and Steven Verschuren.*
*You are my roots.*

—AV

# CONTENTS

# FOREWORD

Annette Verschuren is a great Canadian leader. Having known her for more than three decades, I've long been an admirer of Annette's exceptional leadership qualities, her entrepreneurial expertise and her commitment to the greater good. She's also helped to foster the next generation of leaders, including through the Governor General's Canadian Leadership Conference, which she chaired in 2012 with impressive results.

This is a splendid book that tells Annette's story in her own words. In fact, it is at least four books in one volume. Each is a gem with wide appeal. First, Annette has given us a compelling personal story. The third of five children growing up in a Dutch immigrant farming family in Cape Breton, Nova Scotia, she learned at an early age what it was to work hard and to believe in oneself. Here we see a portrait of an intrepid young girl who would go on to excel in business as a woman pioneering her way in a man's world. Character, energy, resilience and a tenacious optimism shine through in these pages. This is a journey of intriguing personal stories, some humorous, some humane and some hugely challenging. Throughout, we're treated to an instructive view of the road travelled and gain a sense of Annette's infectious optimism and eagerness to tackle new challenges.

The second story within this volume is about leadership. Time and again we witness Annette's intriguing ability to view obstacles as opportunities. From her willingness to make her way in the traditionally male-dominated business world to her insight into the demands of leadership in the twenty-first century, we come to understand the qualities that lie behind her success. They are qualities of teamwork, of self-awareness, of resilience, of creativity and of the ability to learn from failure. One example of these qualities in play can be seen in the story of Annette's current efforts in the innovative field of energy storage. Two other leadership qualities are predominant. One is her focus on the triple bottom line, which aims to balance a return on investment with sustainable development and the creation of social capital. The other leadership quality that stands out is Annette's philosophy and practice of giving back to community and to country. It's an example that has inspired many.

Building on the leadership theme, the third story focuses on the modern organization and the impact of an accelerating pace of change that has seen revolutionary innovations in areas such as retail operations and supply chain management. Instructive lessons can be extrapolated to all manner of modern enterprises and organizations. Annette's stories are candid and own up to past successes and failures alike, including an account of her leadership of Home Depot's unsuccessful venture into China while she was also heading up the company's most successful Canadian division. Her insights and anecdotes are compelling, illustrating the complexity of globalization, and the imperative to understand and integrate local realities, to allow time for success to take root and to constantly nurture skills and talent while navigating change.

The fourth story in this book is a triumphant and inspirational one that speaks to the idea of Canada. It's about a family that chose this country after leaving the Netherlands following the devastation of the Second World War, settled in a challenging landscape and built a successful farm with tenacity, optimism and reliance on friends and family. In this, Annette's story is the story of so many of us. This is a country in which wave after wave of immigrants has arrived with new energy and ideas, creating a richer and more vibrant society in the process. Fairness, hard work, resilience, civility, innovation, openness, the absence of rigid class or hierarchical structures: these are the Canadian values we most celebrate and they are a constant presence in Annette's story. They portray Canada as a smart and caring country.

This book draws the reader in. As I put it down after reading it in one sitting, I thought of a story I'd once heard that took place almost a century ago in England. The setting was an elite London art gallery. On display was an exhibition of some of the first Group of Seven landscape paintings. The paintings were vigorously panned by London's leading art critic. He cited one Tom Thomson work in particular, *The West Wind*, an iconic painting of a lonely pine tree growing out of a rock and leaning at a precarious angle. The critic suggested that this painting had none of the pastoral gentleness, the soft and soothing colours or sense of grace in design of Turner or Constable, the great English landscape painters of the previous century.

In reply, a less-noted but more perceptive critic, who had seen the Canadian landscape first-hand and knew something of the Canadian character, said: "That is just the point. This lonely pine tree emerged from granite. It has had to withstand a severe temperature range from intense summer heat to winter ice. It has had to grow and thrive in gale-force winds. It is tough, creative and resilient, and built around unusual challenges."

That is the nature of Canada, the critic said. These paintings are the essence of the Canadian character.

Similarly, Annette Verschuren has given us a book that reveals something of a smart and caring country. It is told in a highly personal, direct and conversational style, and it stimulates inspired thoughts about the idea of Canada.

*His Excellency the Right Honourable David Johnston*
*Ottawa, September 2015*

# INTRODUCTION

"I think you're going to love it," the office manager told me, moments before we stepped into my plush new digs. It was 1996 and it was my first day on the job as president of Home Depot Canada. I was a thrumming mix of excitement, nerves and surging confidence.

My guide led to me to an imposing black door. He pressed a button, the door swung open and he gestured for me to walk through. He pressed another button just inside the office and, as quiet as you please, the door closed behind us again.

"Well?" he asked, smiling hopefully, "what do you think?"

It was the biggest, grandest office I'd ever seen. And I had seen some grand offices. Five hundred square feet, expensive artwork, full bathroom and shower, no expense spared.

Two thoughts flashed across my mind. The first was that the girl once affectionately known around her hometown as "Poopie" had come a long, long way from the milking stalls of her youth. The second was that, as grand as the office was, it had to go. It was beautiful, it was impressive—It. Just. Wasn't. Me.

I smiled supportively at the office manager and made a beeline for the desk. "Very impressive!" I said. "And I'll probably be making some changes."

A few months later I'd cut my office down drastically. In the space that had once served as a sprawling sitting area, there was a newly constructed meeting room and audiovisual centre available for use by all employees, not just the president. The button that automatically closed the door behind me was gone, as was my cushy parking space closest to the front entrance. The parking lot was now a strictly first-come, first-serve operation. I parked as far from the front doors as possible, and walked through the store that was attached to the head office so that I could connect with as many customers and employees as possible before starting my day.

My actions were seen as inspiring by some, unsettling by others. I wasn't trying to be bold or radical. I was just being authentic. The pulse of any business is on the front lines, where employees and customers meet. I didn't want the trappings of my CEO status—be it a luxury office or a premium parking spot—to insulate me from the people I served, or vice versa. I'd stepped into the biggest job of my life at a time when the business world was entering a period of unprecedented change. Emails were beginning to replace couriers and intra-office memos. Cell phones were fast becoming a non-luxury device. A farm girl from Cape Breton had just been named president of Canada's leading construction and hardware company. The world was changing faster than anyone had anticipated, and I figured that if I was going to succeed, I needed something solid to hang on to. And that solid thing wasn't a title, a legacy or a swanky office. That solid thing was *me*.

Today, I don't have an office, per se. I work at a large board table in an open-concept office with seven of the best and brightest minds in the emerging market of energy storage.

The other day I looked up from some spreadsheets I was reviewing and studied my colleagues' faces. With one notable exception—my right-hand woman, Allison Blunt—every single person at that table was younger than me by a couple of decades. In other words, they were all roughly the age I was when I took the reins at Home Depot. When up-and-comers like the folks who work with me today ask for advice, I most often offer them some variation of what I know to be the essential truth about leadership: Trust yourself. Bet on you, so that others can do the same.

The external pressures of business can feel enormous. I feel privileged to have led many thousands of people, but there are moments when the weight of those responsibilities has been tremendous. Whether you lead a team of a hundred or a team of one (yourself), I know you've felt the pressure too: meeting deadlines, managing a million moving parts, making the right call, choosing the right opportunities at the right time, looking after the people you care about, be they colleagues, customers or employees. To withstand these myriad challenges and stay sane and on track, you need a fixed mark. A benchmark you can rely on. That fixed mark is you. I didn't get where I am today by doubting myself and following orders. I got here by working hard, raising my hand and trusting myself. I bet on myself again and again. You need to do the same.

Nothing about my journey has been easy. Fun, yes. Exhilarating, absolutely. But easy? Not by a long shot. I've been the lone woman in a sea of men more times than I can count. I have led a multibillion-dollar organization through the largest recession since the Great Depression, advised senior politicians on the state of our nation's finances in the wake of the 2008 meltdown, and lived through some of the toughest boardroom politics you can imagine. In other words, I have had a long and satisfying career in the upper echelons of corporate Canada. I led Home Depot's expansion from nineteen Canadian stores in 1996 to 179 when I left almost fifteen years later. As one of North America's few women directors, I have helped steer some of our continent's largest and most influential publicly traded companies. I'm the chancellor of a university. If there's one thing I know how to do, it's how to lead. When I started my career, a person was a leader if he had a title. But dramatic changes of our times have changed all that. As I write this, the United States is experiencing one of the worst droughts in living memory. Wars rage throughout the Middle East and present serious threats to other parts of the world. The sub-prime mortgage fiasco and moral bankruptcy of financial outfits such as Lehman Brothers pulverized the world's economy and badly tarnished the reputation of corporate leadership across all sectors. We are living in murky, complex times that bring to mind a military concept. In peaceful times, an army can thrive with sound leadership at the top and decent managers throughout the ranks. But in the fog of war, strong leadership is required at every level. When I take a hard look at the world we share today, I see a whole lot of fog—and a huge need for stronger leaders in every corner of society.

Our world and the billions of people who inhabit the planet are in danger. Overpopulation and environmental degradation have taken us to the brink of ecological disaster. The old model of doing business—profits over people, growth no matter the cost—is largely to blame. We are on a completely unsustainable trajectory. When I look past the horizon at the kind of leadership the world requires of me, my peers and you, I know that the future is going to require absolutely everything we have, and then some.

That's where you come in. I wrote this book not for my colleagues or peers, but for the emerging leader. Up-and-comers like you, who have big ambitions and want to be a part of the solution our world so badly needs. To reshape the conversation, challenge the status quo, be a part of the change and become the leader you're capable of becoming, you're going to have to bet on yourself time and again. In this book, I'll show you how to do just that.

Here is the good news: You already have everything you need to be exactly the sort of leader the world so desperately needs—values-driven, collaborative, resourceful, responsible, oriented to sustainability. Over my thirty-nine-year career, I have led and worked with teams of all stripes and sizes, from companies employing tens of thousands of people, to units of one or two individuals. I have consulted with presidents and learned from miners, recruited handymen and championed artisans. If you pay attention, a career in corporate leadership offers an unparalleled view into the recesses of the human psyche. And what I know to be true of the human condition is this: under the right circumstances, and given the right support, all of us can become the values-driven, collaborative, resourceful, responsible leaders the world and business both need. We just need to do one hugely important thing: cultivate the internal resources required to trust our instincts, adhere to our values, and take the right course of action.

I grew up in a large farming family in a small town. If there's a situation more likely to keep you humble, I haven't found it. I had a fun- and adventure-filled childhood, but I milked a lot of cows, picked a lot of rocks and shovelled a lot of shit. We kids were allowed to party and have fun, but never until the farm chores were done. Our family's livelihood depended upon our labour. In my community, I knew everyone and everyone knew me. There was no opportunity to put on airs and graces, or to pretend to be anything other than what I was. I had no choice but to be myself one hundred percent of the time.

Being me one hundred percent of the time has paid off. I have had a long and satisfying career in business. I started out as a business developer in an economic development organization with a focus on coal mining, worked for a federal Crown corporation (Canada Development Investment Corporation), then was hired by Canadian corporate legend Purdy Crawford to work on mergers and acquisitions. I formed a joint venture to bring the arts and crafts retailer Michaels to Canada, and in 1996 I was recruited to lead Home Depot in Canada. The company's revenues shot from $660 million when I took over to more than $6 billion when I left. I now run an energy storage start-up.

Over the course of my career, as I moved into increasingly senior roles, I had to work against the stereotype of what women leaders were like, and what we could do. My success didn't happen by accident, nor did I get a lucky break. Time and again I had to dig deep, trust my instincts and bet on myself. As a kid and young woman, I couldn't escape who I was. Over the course of my career, the inevitability of being me blossomed into an enduring self-acceptance. And the more I accepted myself for who I was—strength and limitations alike—the more confidence I was able to build, and the more I was able to relate to, accept and co-operate with others. The more I trusted in myself, the more I was able to inspire loyalty, support and excellence in others. I was willing to bet on myself. And in doing so, I inspired others not only to bet on me, but also (and just as important) to bet on themselves. And so a surprising thing happened. In the supposedly cutthroat, shallow world of business, my commitment to sustainability, serving others and being authentically me led me to a level of success, influence, wealth and fulfillment that I never imagined possible. The companies I led did better financially, environmentally and across many other measures. It sounds simple, but the truth is that staying true to yourself is enormously difficult when faced with the pressures of pleasing your boss, hitting targets and making your customers happy. But, as I'm about to share, the timeless principles I have followed in my career have allowed me to build success for myself and for the people around me. These principles are straightforward. Following them is crucial—especially now.

The great Canadian thinker Marshall McLuhan said, "There are no passengers on spaceship Earth. We are all crew." In this, as in so many other things, McLuhan was right. The challenges we are facing collectively require a new model of doing business, in which the potential of every individual and every department is fully unleashed. We all have to pitch in. The age of silos, blindly following orders and mindless profit hunting are dead and gone. Thanks to rapid social change, globalization, the proliferation of technology and the Internet of Things, a new way of doing business is emerging.

Collaboration, speed, sustainability and communication are critical. And in this new business model, a new type of leadership is required. Becoming the type of leader the world needs— the type of leader capable of ushering in this new model of advancement that marries profitability *and* sustainability— means unleashing who you truly are, and learning how to bring that self into the world of action and execution in a systematic way so that you can bet on yourself over and over again. This book will help you do that. So let's get started.

# CHAPTER 1

# KNOW YOUR BASELINE

I don't have many pictures of myself as a child. Five kids, a busy farm—we were so engaged in living our lives that we didn't have much time to document the process. But there is one photograph that I cherish. It's a faded, grainy, black-and-white picture, but it's me all right. I'm about eight years old and standing in front of the milking stalls in the barn. I've got a bucket in one hand and a milking machine in the other. Arms as muscled as a teenage boy's, bowl-cut blond hair in my eyes and a look of blithe determination on my face. I love that photo because it captures the heart of who I am: strong, independent, happy and not afraid to get my hands dirty.

My life has altered dramatically since that picture was taken. I've traded the cow stalls of Upper North Sydney, Nova Scotia, for the heart of one of the world's busiest financial districts. But I keep that photo near because it reminds me that, in a fundamental way, I haven't changed. That hard-working girl with dung under her fingernails? She's my baseline. And as long as I stay true to her, I know I can't go wrong.

Becoming a leader is one of the most profound professional and personal journeys you can take. The path starts out inno-cently enough. You get a promotion and suddenly you have people reporting to you. They're following you because of your title. Because you're working closely with your team, you have the opportunity to get to know everyone individually. Over time, these close working relationships blossom into a mutual respect that reinforces your leadership, over and above your job title. When this happens, people follow you not because they have to, but because they *want* to. But at some point in your leadership career, you cross a threshold. You simply cannot develop intimate relationships with your entire team, because that team is the size of a small city. Front-line workers don't report to *you* per se; they report to supervisors or managers who are many steps away from your name on the org chart. At that point, leaders who rely on title alone are dead in the water. When you get to that level of leadership, your credibility as a leader comes not from your title or from who you are, but from what you represent. I have witnessed this phenomenon over and over again in authentic leaders of all stripes, from the world of business, politics and social change. I never met Nelson Mandela, but I know what he represented: justice, freedom and perseverance. His unrelenting commitment to his values stood him through his long years in prison, and later helped to amplify his message and vision as a leader. His power was derived neither from his title (he was a prisoner for much of his adult life), nor from who he was (only a tiny fraction of his followers ever actually met the man). His power was rooted in what he represented.

So take a minute and think about it. What do you stand for? If you want to be the kind of leader the world needs now, you've got to be crystal clear on the values you uphold and represent. You've got to know your baseline.

## ESTABLISHING MY BASELINE

In a perfect world, all aspiring leaders would be required to spend a year of their lives on a family farm, milking cows, doing barn chores, plowing fields and shovelling shit. I'm only half joking. I have a degree in business administration and I have had the honour of working with some of the world's greatest business luminaries. Yet I got my introduction to the fundamental principles of leadership on our family farm.

It has been decades since I last milked a cow or drove a hay wagon. (Actually, there's been one notable exception—in 2013 I took part in a cow-milking competition with Mark Eyking, an MP from Cape Breton who just happens to have been raised in one of the island's most prominent farming families. I'm happy to report that at the end of the three-minute hand-milking competition, I had five and a half cups of milk, and he had half a cup.) No matter where in the world I find myself, I only have to close my eyes and *boom!* I'm right back on the farm, standing on the grassy hilltop, the tangy smell of silage and warm milk filling my nose, and a cool breeze blowing up off the harbour.

My parents, Anthony and Annie Verschuren, emigrated from Holland in 1951, part of a wave of Dutch immigrants who settled across Canada. After working for two years in Truro and then another two years on the St. Francis Xavier University farm in Antigonish, they scraped together enough money to buy a one-hundred-acre farm just outside the town limits of North Sydney, Cape Breton. The property had a house in decent condition, an old barn, ten cows and two horses. When my Opa came to visit from Holland, he called his son's farm a "pile of rocks." Pop called it paradise. Mom

called it a whole pile of stuff to get organized. Three fundamentally different viewpoints all coming together in support
of a single vision—making it in the new country. My grand-
father's skepticism helped my parents remain rooted in the real
world. My father's optimism fuelled the long, hard years
required to bring their vision to life. And my mother's pragmatism was the organizing influence they needed to fulfill their
mission. You could say I was baptized into what I now know
to be a highly successful team dynamic: the visionary (Pop),
the organizer (Mom), and the analytical truth teller (Opa).

Over the next decade, my mother would give birth to five
children—me, my sister, Dorothy, and my three brothers:
Turk, Andy and Steven. I was number three. Ask anyone
raised on a farm and they'll tell you that an agricultural childhood is a mix of pure exhilaration and hard labour. *Family
farm* isn't a misnomer; it accurately describes the "all hands
on deck" reality of what is now a fast-disappearing institution.
My parents both left a potentially comfortable, middle-class
life in Holland for a decidedly harder go in Canada.
Throughout my childhood—even after the farm became
better established—there was never much money to go around.
When my siblings and I were very small, Mom wore the same
winter coat for a decade. As we grew up, we became aware, in
the way children do, that we were among the poorest of our
peers. We wore hand-me-down clothes from friends and could
never afford the niceties others enjoyed. But while we seldom
had new threads, we were always clean, our shoes polished and
our clothes ironed. Maybe it was this have-not experience, or
maybe it was something totally inherent in me—either way, I
hatched big plans for myself. When I was seven, I told my

mother that I was going to be "president." President of what, I doubt I knew. Some years later, I'd tell my relatives visiting from Holland that I wanted to be a millionaire. Even though we lived in humble circumstances, my entire family was building something together. The experience inspired in me a desire to dream big, and an understanding that I'd have to overcome obstacles and work hard to get what I wanted.

My parents were practical people with little money to spare, but they bought us toys when they could. I can remember a little buggy they gave us—we called it a "jigger"—that could drive on land and float in water. It was nearly always broken, but we loved fixing it almost as much as we loved riding—and ultimately breaking—it. Life was very, very simple. Mom and Pop wrote letters to family in Holland in which they described their new life in Canada in glowing terms. Maybe a bit too glowing. They were a proud couple and didn't want their parents to worry needlessly. The reality was that our family lived from one milk cheque to another. No saving—just surviving and reinvesting.

As my parents worked to transform the rock pile into a functioning farm, we kids were gradually folded into the mix. We started out clearing land and picking rocks, and graduated to feeding calves, doing simple barn chores and milking cows. Meanwhile, our parents looked for ways to bring extra money into the household. Our neighbour, Mr. Al Lantz, worked as a salesman for L. E. Shaw Ltd., a brick company in Sydney. His company needed temporary help hauling gravel by wheelbarrow to make foundation blocks for houses. Pop took this job for one week when I was very little. He would get up at five to milk the cows, feed the animals, shovel out the manure and take the milk cans to the end of a steep driveway, where they'd be picked up by the dairy truck. Then he'd drive over to L. E. Shaw to start work at nine o'clock. He shovelled gravel all day. At five in the afternoon he would drive back home to do the farm routine, all over again. It was exhausting work but the pay was good and we needed the money. Over the years, Pop picked up odd jobs like this to support us. Mom did her part too. We also took in boarders who were studying at a nearby trade school, and a great deal of Mom's time was spent on the extra work required to house and feed these young men.

Years later, in the early 1980s, my family was instrumental in working with our church parish to sponsor a Vietnamese family to settle in North Sydney. We still had little to spare, but we did our best to ensure the newcomers had the practical support they needed to integrate into their new lives. I was a member of the Parish committee that worked to find jobs, a home, hospital care, et cetera. For many years, they would thank me for the kindness my family showed them and I still receive Christmas cards from them. To this day when I think about our role in supporting that family, I feel a sense of pride. I learned that generosity and helping those in need is a form of currency; my parents taught me that helping others is an honour.

Our parents or caretakers are often the first leaders we encounter. Their example can either lay out how good leadership should or shouldn't work. As I watched Mom and Pop and their unrelenting willingness to do whatever it took to bring their vision to life, while supporting us kids in our own development, my own baseline with respect to leadership emerged. I started to see leadership as a form of service. It was about leading by example *from the trenches*. My parents never once asked us to do something they wouldn't do themselves. They set a powerful example I followed consciously and unconsciously, my entire life.

Because there was so much work to be done, our parents couldn't afford to hold us back or baby us. As soon as we were seventy-five percent capable of doing a job, we were doing it. I was driving the tractor when I was nine years old. Imagine: a nine-year-old driving a tractor! I loved it—the freedom, the challenge, the responsibility. We never got bored on the farm because we were constantly being stretched to do more, try new things, push ourselves just a little beyond what we thought we could easily handle. I learned early on that giving people a big sandbox and lots of room to stretch is an essential part of motivation.

But life wasn't all work. We had a lot of simple pleasures. Our parents planned an outing on the Sunday closest to their anniversary every year. They'd pile us five kids, a full picnic basket, a few toys, blankets and a bar of soap into a little wagon that was attached to the back of the tractor. Pop would drive and Mom would stand on the tractor tire bumper next to him. Off we went to Pottles Lake, which bordered the farthest edge of the farm, all of us breathing in diesel fumes. We'd set up our blankets on the lakeshore and spend hours playing in the water, eating goodies and relaxing. Then a quick bath in the lake so we wouldn't have to have one when we got back home. I'll admit, I get a little twinge of guilt over the phosphates that streamed into the water from our soapy hair but, as you'll see, I made up for it later in my career. Looking back, those days seem like heaven. They didn't cost anything but felt as wonderful to me as any expensive trip ever would. Being together was the important thing. From birth to age eleven, life was pretty much perfect.

And then everything changed.

It was the summer of 1967. Pop was forty-four and hitting his prime. The farm was turning a small profit, which he was reinvesting in the business. He was working especially hard that summer building a new barn. He also wanted to move a small storage building about twenty-five feet to the new barn so he wouldn't have to walk so far carrying the heavy milk cans to the cooler. He had devised a plan to move the building with his brother, my Uncle Cor. He'd use the tractor to pull the building off its foundation onto some strategically placed round logs. Then he planned to roll the building, using the logs as wheels, to its new location. It rained the morning of the move and the logs were wet. In the process, the building slipped off its rollers. I don't know exactly what happened next, but whatever my father did to try to stop the building from slipping was intensely strenuous. He had a massive heart attack, straining his heart muscle, which had already been scarred by pleurisy when he was very young. And just like that, my life changed completely.

## FINDING THE GOOD IN THE BAD

I've noticed that people spend an awful lot of time worrying about catastrophes. What I've learned—beginning with the very first catastrophe I ever experienced, my father's heart attack—is that intense hardship brings out the very best in people.

The doctors told us that there was a fifty percent chance that Pop wouldn't survive. But they were one hundred percent certain that if he lived, he'd never be able to do hard labour again. Farming has changed a lot in forty-eight years, but in those days farming was ninety percent hard labour. Dad's prognosis meant he'd never truly be able to work on the farm again.

Overnight, Mom was left at home with five children under fourteen. Haying season—one of the busiest and most important times on any farm because it is when the feed is harvested that will sustain the cows for the long winter—was a few short weeks away. We kids were capable, but there was no way we could bring the hay in on our own. My uncle and aunt who lived next door helped out when they could, but they had their hands full running their own farm. Nor could we ask other farmers we knew for help; like my relatives, they'd be flat out in their own fields. We couldn't buy feed for the winter because we had no savings. Meanwhile, the cows had to be milked twice a day every day. These were the blunt realities we faced, even as we dealt with the stress of almost losing Pop. It quickly became clear that the only thing standing between us and the poorhouse was my fearless mother and her brood of gangly kids. There were no drawn-out meetings or negotiations. Together we sprung to action. We didn't overthink, we *did*. And that's what saved us.

Mom, my oldest brother, Turk, who was twelve, and I, then eleven, shared the milking duty. We got up every morning at five to milk the cows. Andy fed the calves. Dorothy, who was fourteen, stayed in the house with our youngest brother, Steven, who was only two. Dorothy cooked breakfast, made lunches and dressed the younger children. We had no shower back then, so Turk, Andy and I ate a quick breakfast and washed up before school. In the afternoons we'd come home and follow a similar routine. Weeks passed. Every day Dorothy went to the hospital to visit our father. He was beside himself with frustration that he couldn't help us. Dorothy told him that between Mom, Turk and me, the milking was getting done. His biggest worry was how we were going to bring in the hay.

Then one day there was a knock at our door. Mom opened it to find an old acquaintance of ours, Frank Beaton. Frank had been a district councillor for the area and had met my parents when he was campaigning several years earlier. He and his wife, Joan, had seven children and had once been farmers, though they hadn't been able to make a go of it. So Frank had taken on a government job with a good salary and four weeks' holiday. His daughter, Lorna, was my best friend, and when I wasn't needed on the farm, I would visit her house. He told my mother he'd heard we were in trouble and was there to help us make the hay. Frank spent his entire vacation driving the mower and balers while my siblings and I packed the hay bales in the barn. When my father got out of the hospital a month later, he cried at seeing the barn filled with hay—enough to feed our herd during the cold months. My parents called it a miracle. Without Frank's help, there would have been no way we could have hung on to the farm. To this day, I get emotional thinking about Frank Beaton, and how his act of generosity saved our farm. Today, we focus a great deal of our charity efforts on giving money. Money is a wonderful thing—it makes the world go round. But Frank's deed was a powerful testament to the power of giving something other than money. I have followed his example throughout my career.

Over the next few years, my parents worked together to lead the farm. My mother—the practical, thrifty one—managed the finances. Pop set the direction and made decisions over how we'd spend our time and money. The kids did a lot of the work. I developed ropey muscles and callus-hardened hands. I can remember one year I went trick-or-treating with Andy. We had taken great delight in creating costumes that rendered us totally incognito. When we got to one of our neighbours' houses, he made a great production of trying to figure out who we were. He studied the only parts of us that were exposed— our hands—and declared that we were clearly both boys. I took his candy and said thank you, but I was mad as hell and couldn't understand why Andy thought the episode was so hilarious.

Another reason why I think farming is a great preparation for leadership is that you learn the secret of work-life balance. And the secret is this: Make your work fun. I was always look-ing for ways to make money. It wasn't the money itself that thrilled me; it was the rush of actually *making it*, a rush I enjoy to this day. Although the farm was doing okay, there was never any question of us kids getting paid—my parents simply didn't have the money. So if I was going to get my hands on some cash, I had to do it on my own. There was just one problem: I didn't have the time to work anywhere other than the farm, which took a good four hours of my time each and every day. So I came up with a plan: I'd start babysitting, like other girls my age. But rather than babysit kids at their houses, I brought them over to the farm and "watched" them while I did my chores. I babysat a few different neighbourhood kids, but two girls stick out in my memory, Belinda and Paula Fiander.

The Fianders owned a building supplies store in town. During the summer months, when Paula and Belinda were off school, their parents' business went through its high season and they needed someone to look after their six-and nine-year-old daughters. When they brought them to the farm, they probably thought we'd play dolls and bake cookies. Not even close. I'm sure Paula and Belinda would have enjoyed such activities, but I gave them something even better—an adventure. I taught them how to feed milk to baby calves, I sat them on top of the hay wagon while my siblings and I threw up the bales, I took them for tractor rides. My reality was this: I had to work on the farm, and I also wanted to earn some money. So I put the two together. The truth is, though I grumbled about my years of unpaid labour—as any child in my situation would—I enjoyed farm work. I also loved babysitting the Fiander girls and wanted them to enjoy our time together. So I did my best to make our work time fun. Years later, I'm still friends with the Fianders, and while they don't remember the work, they remember the fun. Making it fun allowed us to keep the farm going while I took on extra work. Plus, I got free help. And in this seemingly simple childhood example, I learned yet another powerful lesson—the importance of fun and enthusiasm. If you can lay out a vision and create an atmosphere that is positive and fun, people will be more productive, efficient and they'll follow you to the ends of the earth.

You might not consider yourself to be a naturally "fun person." Planning a party might be your personal definition of hell. That's okay. Fun doesn't have to be about pyjama parties and cocktails (as great as those things are). You can increase your fun factor by doing three simple things. First, by cultivating a positive, upbeat attitude when you work with other people. Second, by taking every opportunity you can to demonstrate authentic care for other people's well-being. This might be as simple as ensuring they are totally comfortable when they meet with you and always remembering to offer them something to eat or drink. And third, by trying to invite people into your world in some way so that you bring your relationship outside the strict limits of the office.

Here's an example. I work in Toronto, but my heart is and forever will be in Cape Breton. My true home is a log house on the shores of the Bras d'Or Lake. Each summer, I invite my close colleagues over to stay with my husband, Stan, and me in our home. Last summer we hosted a senior executive of a major company whose board I sit on, as well as some colleagues with whom I have worked for years. We hiked, took road trips, swam and kayaked. We had fun. Sharing this bond of fun will make it so much easier for us to work together productively later. People in business have a lot of rules about how to associate with colleagues—we may have been raised with the belief that work is work, play is play, and the two should be kept strictly separated. I think this mindset interferes with the ability to have and to be fun. Looking for occasional opportunities to involve colleagues in things you enjoy is a great way to cement your bonds and personal effectiveness, with other people.

## BUILDING RESILIENCE THROUGH CHALLENGE

I'm fascinated by people and by the way in which our personalities form and re-form over time. I think we all have innate qualities that can be nurtured and honed through experience. The ability to take risks is an essential quality for a leader. If you were to ask people who know me well to describe me, "risk taker" would be one of the first things they'd say. I come by my risk-taking qualities honestly. As a child, I often found myself in challenging situations that I had to learn to handle on my own. Dairy cows aren't known to be aggressive animals, but when you're a seventy-pound child working in close quarters with one of those creatures, you quickly learn how to calculate risk, and how to operate in the presence of risk. I don't have children of my own, but I gather that childhood has changed a great deal in the last fifty years. Children today don't experience the freedom I did growing up. I understand the desire to keep children close in a seemingly dangerous world, but I also know that understanding how to calculate risk is a lifelong lesson that is best started early.

I can remember a time from my childhood when I probably came much closer to serious risk than I fully realized. It was a summer day and I was playing by myself in a secluded part of the farm. I was probably eight or nine years old. It must have been a Sunday because I was wearing a dress. A young man who was boarding with us walked up to me and tried to flip up my dress. I kept pulling it down again. While I didn't understand what he was trying to do, I knew in my gut it was wrong. When he wouldn't quit tugging at my dress, I ran to the house and told Dorothy. When my parents came home from church and heard the story, they sent the man packing. What I remember of the experience was a deep sense of confidence and self-reliance. I was afraid, yet I'd had the courage to run and use my voice to protect myself. This episode reinforced my confidence in my abilities. I learned that courage always precedes confidence.

My teenage years took my appetite for risk to whole new levels. I partied hard with my brother Turk. My poor parents! I remember Turk and I stumbling up the stairs at ungodly hours, and then stumbling down a few hours later to do the milking. I worked hard and played hard. I learned to work fast and well so that I'd have more free time and would never be called home to redo a job. My siblings all worked hard, and as much as they enjoy razzing me we all agree: I was the fastest milker. As a kid, I'd enter 4H milking competitions and win them all. A little competition not only makes you better, it also makes the experience more enjoyable. Besides, the faster I got the milking done, the sooner I'd be able to head to my extracurricular activities. Basketball was my sport. I just loved getting onto the court, forgetting about schoolwork and the farm, being completely immersed in the game. The problem was that as I started to sweat, the smell of cow dung—which after six years of twice-daily milkings was well and truly ground into my skin—became magnified thanks to my body heat. One day I was bringing the ball down the court during a scrimmage. One of my teammates called for the ball. But rather than using my name, she yelled, "Hey, Poopie!" We had to stop the scrimmage for a minute because my teammates were laughing so hard. I laughed along, too. The girl who yelled it wasn't a bad person, but in truth her comment cut me. I used every brand of soap, every home remedy you can think of to get the smell off, and nothing worked. So, at age sixteen, the height of teenage insecurity, I had a brand new nickname: Poopie.

From that day forward, my schoolmates might have been able to smell me sweat, but they sure didn't see it. I never batted an eyelash during the daily occasions that people used that name. But every time I heard someone call me that name, I made a silent vow that one day I'd show those kids what

Poopie was really made of. I laugh about it now, but back then I was dead serious.

Years later, my mentor, Purdy Crawford—a Canadian business icon who figures prominently in my story—would tell me the number one quality he looked for in a leader. "You have to have that fire in the belly," he said. The hardships of farm life, and of my humiliating nickname, ignited a simmering wildfire that wouldn't die down for years.

## REFLECTING ON YOUR DEFINING MOMENTS

During one of my basketball games, I took a hard hit to the back. I doubled over in pain and had to sit out the rest of the game. No one thought anything of it, even me. I was sixteen years old, and before long I'd be as good as new, we figured. Except I didn't get better. I got worse. Over the next few weeks, I became so ill I could barely get out of bed. My parents took me to the hospital in North Sydney. I stayed there for more than a week as the doctors tried to figure out what was wrong with me. None of the treatments they gave me worked—my body was starting to shut down. My temperature was 104, I couldn't pee, I couldn't move. I remember the nurses laying me in a bath of ice in order to bring my temperature down.

Then one morning a new doctor performed the morning rounds. He was from Montreal and had a terrible stutter. He came through with the nurse and stopped in front of my bed. I remember him studying me—really *looking* at me. Then he looked at my chart. He turned to the nurse. "We need to X-ray her kidneys." It took a good minute to get the sentence out. The X-rays were done that morning. Twelve hours later I was on the operating table. My entire system was poisoned. The doctor had discovered that my urinary tract was completely filled with cysts. Because I wasn't able to flush liquid toxins, they had become trapped in my body, damaging my kidney and urethra. The first operation was to clean out the damaged tissue. Then he ordered my parents to take me home and get my iron count up so that he could do a second operation.

So it was liver for breakfast, lunch and dinner. Liver seventy thousand different ways. A few weeks later my iron count was high enough for the second operation. I was too sick to feel scared. I remember going under, and then all was darkness. When I woke up a few hours later, I immediately started throwing up. Puking and tearing at my stitches, I was in profound pain and delirious. I remember a nurse forcing me down and pushing a breathing tube into my throat. I was vomiting so intensely I couldn't breathe. The last thing I remember before passing out was this thought flashing through my mind: *I want to die.*

The next few days passed in a haze of misery and unconsciousness. I am a profoundly optimistic person. But because of my health crisis, I know what it is to be so miserable that you lose the will to live. And in truth, I came incredibly close to death. When I finally regained consciousness, my entire family was jammed into the hospital room. My father was standing at the foot of the bed. "Annette, when I was sick you were there to help me. Now you're sick and I can't do anything," he said.

For the first and one of the very few times in my life, I saw my father cry. Then everybody was crying—my sister and brothers, my mother, even Nurse Taylor, who was in the room with us. All of us sobbing our hearts out. They cried harder when I told them the doctor had said I wouldn't ever be able to have children. In fact, the only silver lining was that he'd honoured my request that I'd be able to wear a bikini. He made the neatest incisions you can imagine on both sides of my rib cage.

When visiting hours were over and my family went home, I got some time to think. I felt sorry for myself for about fifteen minutes. Then it dawned on me that I was alive. I'd almost died, but I'd made it. I had experienced misery so deep that I no longer wanted to live, and I had pushed through. And there I was. To this day, I think of the moment I woke up in the recovery room, so wretched that I wanted it all to be over. I became profoundly conscious that I had a choice before me. I could be the person my family felt sorry for, or I could choose to become a truly positive influence—the sort of person others *want* to be around. That wish became my new baseline. Time and again throughout my career, when I've found myself in a difficult or even downright awful situation, I've remembered a time I felt far worse. And I've used that girl's courage to pull me through. If I did it once, I can do it again, I tell myself.

## GETTING CLEAR ON YOUR BASELINE

I'm a storyteller and I love taking a trip down memory lane. But my reason for telling you about my childhood isn't purely for entertainment. I believe childhood is the most formative stage of our lives. Many of our habits, expectations and beliefs are formed before we graduate from high school. Some of us look back and remember our childhoods with fondness. People who had difficult childhoods may attempt to forget the past entirely. For an aspiring leader, neither habit is helpful. Self-awareness and leading oneself are critical building blocks in the formation and evolution of any great leader. As such, we need to look back on our formative experiences not to romanticize, demonize or re-experience them but, more practically, to understand how these experiences shaped us. If you don't have a handle on who you truly are, you can't lead anyone.

The fundamental principles I explore in this book derive from powerful lessons I learned early on in life. While great leaders share common values, they express those values differently. By understanding my values—my baseline—I can not only project these values, I can also align myself with organizations that also hold these values dear. My pragmatic Dutch parents and heritage taught me that actions speak louder than words. A childhood of farm labour taught me the inherent value of good work, and that daily actions create transformative results. My father's heart attack taught me the importance of taking responsibility. Working side-by-side with my parents and siblings taught me the power of *we* before *I*. Teenage cruelty and the experience of poverty ignited a fire in my belly. My near-death experience taught me what it means to truly suffer and recover, a lesson in perspective I have drawn from my entire life. I explore all of these themes—and more—over the course of this book. These are my lessons, my values, my baseline. They are the root of who I am and how I function in the world. Taking the time to truly understand myself and my values has been profoundly important to my professional success.

That's *my* story. But now I want to turn things over to you. What's *your* baseline? What do you know to be fundamentally true? What personal values do you live by?

This might sound a bit woo-woo, but I assure you that taking the time to focus inward and carefully consider these questions is one of the most important things you will ever do. My thirty-nine-year career has seen me consistently log sixty-hour weeks, travel to all corners of the world, lead huge teams of people and face incredibly difficult circumstances. I have operated for four decades in a world of rapid change. You will do the same. In order to get results and be the leader that people actually follow and collaborate with, I had to have a strong foundation. My foundation is my baseline. When I am overwhelmed or facing a crisis, I always return to my core values to give me the emotional strength, certainty and decisiveness of a leader. I advise you to do the same.

## KEY CONCEPTS

1 By identifying values—your baseline—you not only consistently project these values, but you are also easily able to align yourself with organizations that reflect these same values, resulting in a more meaningful and satisfying career.

2 Taking the time to truly understand yourself and your values is profoundly important to your professional success.

3 Knowing and consciously embodying your core values gives you the emotional strength, certainty and decisiveness of a credible leader that others will follow.

# CHAPTER 2

# NOT GOOD, NOT BAD, ONLY BETTER

When I was seven, I was nearly killed in a car accident.

We'd had a huge snowstorm overnight that had cleared up by morning. My family were devout Catholics—missing mass was a mortal sin, no matter what the weather—so we got ourselves ready for church bright and early. Pop was away, so my uncle and aunt picked up Turk, Dorothy and me on their way. Our farm was at the top of a steep hill, and the railway track crossed the road to our house halfway down. Because of the way the road was built, the railway crossing amounted to a blind crest; it was nearly impossible to see a train coming. No one heard the train barrelling down the track, and by the time my uncle, who was driving the car, did notice the train, it was too late. The lane was covered in ice. We collided with that train. The impact threw my aunt out of the car and into a nearby snow bank. We were dragged a few hundred feet. Luckily, we all lived. The only thing I really remember is waking up in an ambulance, wondering how it came to pass that I had gotten blood all over my Sunday best.

None of us felt safe on the road after the accident. What was especially worrying was that we often crossed the railway tracks with our tractor—a slow, noisy machine that in my mother's estimation was a tragedy waiting to happen. When I was thirteen years old, I decided to take matters into my own hands. I typed out a letter to the local Canadian National Railway official explaining how dangerous the railway track was, and that our farm couldn't expand because of it. When I was finished the letter, I gave it to Pop, and asked him to proofread it, and to sign it in his own name. I mailed it off, hoped for the best and, because I was a busy kid, promptly forgot all about it.

A few months later, an official from CNR contacted the Department of Highways and requested that the road be diverted so that it would now run parallel to the tracks, which would allows for a safer crossing. I'll never forget the afternoon that my family and I gathered around to watch the roadwork. The CNR official came over to speak to my father. "That was a good letter you wrote," he said.

Pop pointed to me. "I signed the letter. But she wrote it." I don't think I ever smiled so big. And it took the railway official more than a split second to pick up his chin off the road.

I wasn't the only one who got a kick out of the railway man's expression. The look of pride on my father's face was something I'll hold close for my entire life. Four decades later, I still feel a little surge of pride when I drive up to the old farmhouse, owned now by my brother Turk. When my car wheels bump over the railway tracks (now a very safe crossing), I'm reminded of one of the first times I learned that I could take on a seemingly impossible situation and make it better.

There are so many life lessons wrapped up in that story: the importance of empowering children, giving credit where credit is due. But for me, the most powerful lesson is the belief in making things better. I decided to take ownership and find a way to make a dangerous problem better. The experience taught me that, even at thirteen, I could be a leader. And it taught me that focusing on getting better is one of the most important mindset qualities a leader can adopt. A big part of building the confidence you need to trust yourself, and to keep betting on yourself time and again, is being willing to learn and improve. You have to be willing to focus on getting better. It's a lesson I had to relearn shortly after taking the reins at the biggest job of my career.

## LEARNING TO LISTEN TO CRITICISM

In 1998, less than two years into my tenure as CEO of Home Depot Canada, I sat through my first 360-degree performance evaluation. This type of evaluation was practically unheard of in Canada at that time. More usually, your boss evaluated your performance across a number of key indicators once a year. The whole process happened privately. Just you and your boss sitting in an office or boardroom, going over your work. It was clean and quick. At the conclusion of the meeting, you either got a raise, some pointers and a slap on the back or you got fired. Period. But the 360-degree review blew the established review process wide open. Evaluation was no longer a one-on-one discussion between you and the person you reported to. It was you in front of a panel of people, including direct reports and peers. You got far more than a back slap or a dismissal—you got reams of direct and sometimes downright cutting feedback. There was nothing clean and quick about it.

My first 360 happened in the boardroom at Home Depot's Canadian headquarters. The company had hired a U.S.-based facilitator to come in and lead the process. He in turn had assembled a group of ten people, including my reports and peers, first thing in the morning. They had all filled out written evaluations of my performance, and he had taken them through a small-group discussion to debrief their findings. He brought me into the mix mid-morning. I remember walking into the room with my head held high and a huge smile on my face. I had no reason to be nervous, I thought. I was doing a great job—better than great, in fact. Home Depot was already exceeding its expansion targets.

I took my place at one end of the boardroom table and prepared to accept graciously the praise I felt certain was coming. The facilitator smiled warmly and then turned to the group of ten. "Okay, everyone. Let's tell Annette what she can do to be a better leader."

In the awkward silence before the first person raised his voice, I had a moment of confusion. These reviews normally started with everything I was doing *right* . . . right? My misunderstanding was quickly cleared up as, one after another, my evaluators broke the bad news.

"Annette doesn't spend enough time with me in my development," said one report.

"Sometimes Annette makes decisions without taking into account certain elements of the business," said a colleague.

"Annette favours certain people on her team," said someone else.

For fifteen minutes, I could barely speak. My heart was hammering inside my chest, my breathing was shallow and

I'm sure my face was eight different shades of red. I was hurt and humiliated by what I interpreted to be criticisms of my performance, and I was doing my utmost not to take their feedback personally. As a woman in leadership, I'd experienced my share of snide remarks and tough meetings, but this one took the cake. It felt very personal. Yet every time I opened my mouth to fire back, I thought of my father. He was, and remains, the greatest leader I ever met. And one of the things that made me love him so much was his willingness to be humble and to listen. Sitting in that chair, I tried my best to channel his energy. Two words kept coming to me: *Be humble.* I took a deep breath, refocused on the panel and did my best.

After another fifteen minutes, my breathing and heart rate had slowed and I was able to hear what people were saying. And rather than facing a firing squad out to nail a "bad" leader, I realized I was hearing direct feedback from a group of my co-workers who were not attempting to get me fired but were, in fact, trying to make me a better leader. Was it a tough pill to swallow? Absolutely. I was not born without an ego. But shifting my focus ever so slightly out of the good-versus-bad mindset and into an improvement mindset, helped me enormously. Gradually, I was able to hear more and more of what they had to say. When I walked out of that meeting, I got a slap on the back *and* a list of ten specific things I could do to improve as a leader.

I can remember that list as if I still had it in my back pocket. They told me I needed to spend more time individually with people on my team. I needed to do a better job of listening to everybody—not just the people who were good at playing the game. I learned which decisions needed to be communicated broadly and which could be made quietly. Over the next twelve months, I humbled myself, keeping a mental checklist of my weak points and trying each day to take some definitive action to improve. I made a conscious effort to listen first and talk last. I invited colleagues or reports I didn't know so well for lunch in order to strengthen my relationships with the quieter, more reserved members of my team. I became more consultative, and tried to take into account the needs and opinions of various department heads before making decisions.

By nature, I'm impulsive, decisive and an action taker. Speed has always been important to me—remember, you're talking to a champion milker. In the beginning, slowing down and taking a quieter, more consultative approach felt unnatural. But I made a commitment to myself that I'd try it for a year.

In the end, it took a few months of conscious effort for me to enhance (if not transform) my approach. There were definitely moments that my speak and shoot first/listen and aim second nature came through. About a week after that painful performance review, we had one of our regular team meetings. Our real estate manager was halfway through recommending a new site when I cut him off. "Nope. I don't like it," I said. I was about to chip in with my own recommendation when I caught a pointed look from a colleague who'd been a part of the 360, and realized my mistake.

"I'm sorry," I told the real estate manager. "I didn't give you a chance. Let's try that again." He took the time to carefully outline the benefits of the site. We asked him lots of questions, and eventually we agreed to proceed. His recommendation— the one I so nearly shut down—had been to open a location at Gerrard Square, a small shopping centre in Toronto's east end. It became one of Home Depot's strongest stores.

Over the course of the next year, I made a point of spending time one-on-one with individual team members following team meetings, and I always asked for feedback. It was a humbling experience—there was always something I could improve—but eventually I started to have fun with it. It became a big game of "Who Can Catch Annette at Her Old Ways." But keeping things light and humorous made it so much easier for me to be flexible and change.

The following year I came back for my next 360-degree review. Although I exhibited less swagger than I had the year before, I walked into what is always a challenging situation with a richer, more authentic confidence. Because I had devoted myself to being humble, listening and seeking feedback, I had a stronger sense of how I was perceived. No surprises. At the end of the ninety-minute session, I walked out the door with a much shorter list of behaviours to correct than in the previous year. As my evaluators came one by one to shake my hand and congratulate me, I was reminded that great leaders don't fixate on being bad or good. They focus first on being better. Focusing on being better is the first step in effecting tangible, positive change. And getting *results* is what ultimately gives a leader her power.

## USING VULNERABILITY AS YOUR POINT OF POWER

I've noticed that emerging leaders are sometimes uncomfortable with the concept of power because they equate the term with authoritarianism. Authoritarians—and I've seen plenty of them who run not only countries but also companies—gain a position of dominance through fear. They are unwilling to be vulnerable in any way. But true leaders derive their power through their ability to influence. And at what point do we, as leaders, have the most ability to influence? When we are trying to make things better. And when we are trying to become better, we are also making ourselves vulnerable. It's the only way we can let our guard down long enough to truly learn.

For a full fifteen minutes during my first 360-degree review, I was powerless—I could barely speak, I was a nervous wreck. I completely gave my power away, because I was obsessed with how I would defend myself against the panel's "criticisms." I was totally fixated on proving that I was a "good" leader. Nothing changed for me until I was willing to humble myself. Only when I was able to listen to the feedback I was receiving and *consider how it might be true* could I start imagining how I might use it to make me a better leader. It was in this process of releasing my attachment to being "good" or "bad," and focusing on how to be *better*, that I actually regained my power.

This was a profound lesson for me, but it didn't come easily. My career is littered with examples of (temporarily) getting locked up over the "right" decision—sometimes in defiance of other people.

At one point, I decided that Home Depot should have carpeted floors in the flooring department. (If this horrifies you, I humbly suggest you remember this was the 1990s. Some people even had carpeted bathrooms!) I personally liked carpet, and I felt soft floors offered a better shopping experience, particularly for women. A number of store managers strongly disagreed, but I dug in. I was passionate about the carpets. Carpeted floors became my mission. Flash forward a few years later, and these same stores had started looking a little shabby—the carpets just couldn't stand up to the enormous foot traffic and the weight of forklifts and other equipment used to stock inventory and maintain the store. I wanted to replace the carpets. But the rest of the team decided it was best to get rid of the carpeting and go with polished concrete instead. I remember feeling annoyed and outnumbered. I'd taken such a stand for the carpets, and I worried that backing down would make me look weak. But my colleagues were adamant and I had to remind myself to lead with vulnerability and stand down.

Despite the fact that the carpeting had been popular with customers, after the change sales didn't go down and we received very few complaints. The stores were far easier to maintain with polished concrete floors. I learned that overattachment to personal bias harms good decision making. I learned that listening doesn't just mean "not talking." It also means being willing to let go of things you are attached to or emotionally invested in.

In the circles I travel in, phrases like "releasing attachment to personal bias" raise more than a few eyebrows. I say it anyway, because I see far too many people wearing the Good/Bad blindfold—seeing reality as a series of false dichotomies. And this Good/Bad blindfold is killing the ability to innovate and collaborate at a time in human history when we need innovation and inspired leadership more than ever before.

## UNDERSTANDING POLARIZATION:
## GOOD/BAD'S SNEAKY SIBLING

One of the most powerful leaders in Washington, D.C., wasn't an elected official at all. Katherine Graham was born into a wealthy family and inherited the *Washington Post* following her husband's suicide in 1963. She'd spent most of her life as a stay-at-home mother and for many years after taking the helm of the *Post*, she doubted her abilities as a leader. But she did not doubt her abilities as a hostess, and over the course of her two-decade tenure as publisher she hosted numerous cocktail parties at her Georgetown home, where she invited politicians from both sides of the floor. A few years after her death in 2001, Vernon Jordan, a key member of the U.S. civil rights movement and a close advisor to former president Bill Clinton, told an audience that her passing left a social vacuum in Washington. With no venue or cause to mingle, engage in civil, friendly debate and share ideas, politicians from the right and left gradually drifted back to their own sides. And this vacuum contributed to the current state of what I consider to be almost unprecedented partisanship in American politics.

Polarization is a form of the Good/Bad blindfold. And it is deeply ineffective. In my experience, the further you get from centre, the more ineffectual you become. Case in point: a colleague told me that at a recent talk he attended by world-renowned environmentalist David Suzuki, a prominent Canadian investor stood up and announced to the crowd, "There is no such thing as global warming." Given the staggering amount of information that clearly points otherwise, the audience was flabbergasted that a prominent entrepreneur would take such an extreme position. According to those who were at the event, Suzuki didn't acknowledge the comment, but ignored the investor and moved on to the next question. By taking such a polarizing stance, the investor lost his influence.

Genuine progress happens at the centre. In fact, I believe that polarization lies at the heart of one of the world's most troubling business issues—environmental sustainability. There is a prevailing belief that we need to choose between the bottom line and our environmental footprint. Depending on which stance most captures your feelings, the environment or the bank account, one side is "good" and the other is "bad." And this polarization prevents us from seeing the way forward.

In my new role as CEO of an energy storage company, I live and breathe energy markets. The recent research I have seen suggests that, even if the world gets really aggressive in its targets for renewables, in a decade or so we would still see only five to six percent of energy derived from non-fossil fuels. That's simply the reality. So any movement to eradicate our reliance on "bad" fossil fuels and instead depend on "good" renewable energy is misguided. A more effective path would be to increase our investment in renewable energy technology, conserve energy and find ways to extract, process and burn fossil fuels more efficiently. In this way, we could make genuine progress faster. While the Good/Bad blindfold wearers yell at one another from either end of the stadium, the true leader must be willing to grind it out in the centre of the playing field, working with reality in order to find solutions. "Good" or "bad" I can't work with. The quest for "better," however, is something that I can refine until the cows come home. I know in my heart, and from my experience, that the quest to be better can have enormous environmental impact.

## GREENING HOME DEPOT

The construction industry has never been an environmental darling. Chances are good that if you were alive during the 1980s and '90s, you saw multiple stories on the suppertime news involving showdowns between environmentalists and loggers. Sometimes environmentalists chained themselves to

trees or blockaded logging roads. I always had empathy for
each side, and I believed there was a place for both. Maybe it's
my Dutch heritage—I'm an enduring pragmatist. I saw that
we required lumber and that we also needed to protect our
forests. I never regarded the logging and preservation camps
as an either/or proposition. And when I was president of Home
Depot, I finally had an opportunity to do something about it.

In 1999, years before "green procurement" had made its way
into everyday business jargon, Home Depot announced its
Wood Purchasing Policy, under which we committed to elim-
inating by 2002 wood purchases from regions of the world that
had endangered forests. I chaired the Environmental Council
of the firm at the request of founder Arthur Blank, and as a
council we were committed to using our purchasing power
responsibly. We also made a commitment to sourcing our
lumber from forests that were sustainably managed. As one of
the world's largest purchasers of lumber, I saw first-hand that
our actions could bear powerful and positive results. A few
years later Walmart introduced its own green procurement
policies. Over the next decade, Home Depot Canada went on
to unveil many new green procurement reforms, including
Mow Down Pollution, where four-cylinder gas-powered
mowers could be traded in for a $100 credit toward an electric
mower. We also did promotions for low-flow toilets, and
invited customers to trade in their old incandescent holiday
lights for new LED lights. Each of these actions created positive and tangible environmental results.

There were pundits who argued we could be doing more,
and others who said we were doing all we could do. To me,
many of those arguments were of the Good/Bad blindfold

variety—certain to get your blood pressure up, but not a whole lot more. I pushed to use our significant leverage as a large company to do better. By focusing on continuously getting better, we were able to make significant progress toward uniting profitability and environmental sustainability, which I believe should be among the chief ambitions of the next generation of leaders.

## A GUIDE TO CULTIVATING THE GET BETTER MINDSET

The quest to be better is one that great leaders don't pursue only for their organizations, but also for themselves. Although the surgeries I had on my kidneys as a teenager saved me from dying, I have spent many of my adult years in poor health. My damaged kidneys couldn't process toxins properly, so I took antibiotics daily until I was forty-four. Imagine: the entire time I was building up a national arts and crafts store chain and leading Canada's largest home improvement retailer, I was battling nearly constant bouts of poor health. There were times when I'd come home late at night from a week-long trip across Canada, tumble into bed, and arrive at the office for 7 A.M. the next day, jet-lagged, weak, ill, but still functioning. My medications helped me, but I believe what allowed me to not only function but also to excel during those long years was my commitment to being as healthy as a so-called sick person could possibly be. I'd been told for years that my kidneys were shot and that I could look forward to a lifetime of poor health. I did experience that poor health for years, though I did not lose much time at work. But I made a commitment not to give in to the "bad" diagnosis. A part of me knew that I could do better, if only I found a way.

In my forties, I decided to hire a personal trainer and nutritionist, Larysa Osmak. Over the following decade, I worked out with Larysa as much as I could. Larysa worked primarily with executives, and she told me that few were able to commit to personal training for very long. It's understandable. You work out regularly for a few weeks and you feel great. Then you travel for six weeks—lots of big dinners, sitting in planes, jet lag—and you feel as though you've lost any health gains you originally made. Staying in great health begins to feel like a losing battle—so maybe you quit.

Except that I didn't quit. If I showed up at the gym with Larysa after two weeks in China, I usually felt about half as strong as I did when I left. But I didn't let it bother me. I got to work. Because getting better is a never-ending process. And it always starts by accepting exactly where you are right now.

In time, I asked Larysa to develop specialized meal plans tailored to my demanding travel schedule. My husband supported me tremendously by taking on the task of preparing nutritious meals—something I'd never really managed to do, given my work schedule. Slowly but surely, my health increased. I lost weight, gained energy and started sleeping more.

My health is so much better now. And this in turn has given me the energy I need to run a start-up company, which, though smaller than the previous company I led, is every bit—if not more—demanding.

I have seen way too many leaders literally kill themselves for their careers, sacrificing their health for a few extra minutes at the office. I am a firm believer in putting the time in—I've worked sixty-hour weeks for decades. But I make my health an absolute priority. I don't just feel better when I'm eating well, sleeping soundly and exercising regularly; I think more clearly, and bring more energy and vibrancy wherever I go.

I'll admit that the idea of putting my health and well-being first is easier now than at the beginning of my career. There's no doubt I have a much more demanding schedule now than I did when I was twenty-five. But I'm more empowered now than I was then. If I want to leave the office early for a workout, I can, without having to ask permission. But the ability to put my health first isn't just a matter of being a CEO and being able to call the shots. Times have changed. We are now entering a time of unprecedented awareness about the importance of health. Last year, one of the world's most powerful women, Arianna Huffington, published a book, *Thrive*, which explored the critical importance of health and well-being, which she described as the "third metric" of success, in addition to money and power. I applaud Arianna and other heavy-hitters for using their voices and platform to draw attention to the critical importance of paying attention to one's health. It's harder to bet on yourself if you're two steps away from heart attack or a nervous breakdown. Taking care of yourself is a foundational activity for leaders.

This will be easy for you if you belong to the one percent of the population who always puts health first, has a spacious daily calendar and a boss who is willing to give you an extra-long lunch so that you can attend a CrossFit class. For the other ninety-nine percent, putting your health first will require a little more discipline. I explore time management in a later chapter, but for now I'll say this: I have learned that in order to take care of the most important things in life—things that are often not urgent—I need to put them first. Exercise and adequate sleep may not feel urgent, but they are incredibly important. Prioritize them.

## CULTIVATING A BETTER MIND

One of the smartest people I know, my sister Dorothy, had a mental breakdown when we were both in our forties. I didn't know much about depression or mental illness at the time. The hidden gift in any illness is that it often strengthens the family bond. It certainly did for Dorothy and me. Up to that point, she'd always been my big sister and biggest supporter. In the time we spent together as she healed, she became my best friend. She's an incredible teacher and school administrator, she graduated at the top of her university class, married her high school sweetheart and raised two beautiful boys, all while inspiring thousands of students. She has long been an inspiration to me, and it was challenging to watch her battle depression, but rewarding to support her through it. As Dorothy regained her equilibrium, I came to learn a great deal about mental health in general and depression in particular. But one of the lessons that had the most impact on me is that even those of us without a "mental illness" per se have to be vigilant about taking care of our most precious asset: our minds.

Today it's common for leaders to work with executive coaches. But in the 1990s, when I first started seeing an organizational psychologist, Dr. Cindy Wahler, to talk about life, work and leadership, it was a rarity. When I told friends what I was up to, I got a lot of alarmed looks. But I kept seeing her. Because I understood that it's almost impossible to truly *see* yourself on your own—you need other people to reflect your thoughts and ideas back to you, so that you can give them the level of scrutiny they deserve.

Part of getting better is to become a student of you. As the leader of a large company, you become a figurehead—a larger, technicolour version of yourself. And just like a big boat in a harbour, you create a lot of wake. When I was at Home Depot, there was always excitement when I visited a new store. Everyone watching the president. I always made a point of taking complete responsibility for my wake in those moments, because every little comment I made would be treated with a special gravitas. I couldn't allow myself to stew over a colleague's behaviour or a deal that wasn't going my way. I had to cultivate a very high level of self-awareness in order to be able to generate the kind of positive impact a leader needs to have. Actively managing my thoughts and working on my mind and myself, with the help of mentors and coaches, helped me do that.

## WHAT THIS MEANS FOR YOU

The good news is that the fact you are reading this book indicates you care about improvement—you're likely reading this to pick up some tips and insight in order to become a better leader. I'm often asked how a person can become better at leadership. It's a fair question, but misguided. I believe that if you truly want to improve, you should focus first on leading with humility. Ask yourself, What can I learn here? How can I humble myself enough in order to find the lesson in this person, situation or experience? Humility is always the starting point for improvement. And a focus on improvement—as opposed to good or bad—is mission critical in building businesses and careers that are profitable *and* sustainable.

## KEY CONCEPTS

1   Great leaders don't fixate on being bad or good. They focus on being better. Focusing on getting better is the first step in effecting tangible, positive change. And getting *results* is what ultimately gives a leader her power.

2   Polarization harms the ability to innovate and, ultimately, to remain relevant and competitive.

3   Prioritize your physical, mental and emotional well-being.

CHAPTER 3

# FORGET THE BEST-LAID PLANS

People often ask me how I make decisions. It's a fair question—decisiveness is the hallmark of a strong leader. The desire to understand the process by which powerful CEOs call the shots is the subject of entire MBA courses devoted to individual and organizational decision making.

But when it comes to figuring out *how* to make a decision, I find many people are off base. They spend far too much time and energy conducting research *before* a decision is made because they don't want to make a poor choice. They're afraid of taking a chance and being wrong. So they order up assessments, conduct interviews and reread case studies in an effort to get the information they need to make the "right" choice or the "good" decision.

It's easy to get caught up in paralysis by analysis, even when you know better. But trusting your instincts is a lesson you may have to teach yourself over and over again. At least that has been my experience. Take a recent example at NRStor. A good chunk of our work involves creating energy storage projects (using different technologies, based on the requirements) in response to a government-issued request for proposal (RFP). In 2014, our team was preparing a series of proposals in response to one such government-issued request. I had a number in mind, a price that would not only potentially win us the contracts, but also give us a healthy profit. Most experienced business people will, over time, develop a sense for their particular business's "sweet spot" number, a price that satisfies both buyer and seller. Our investors thought, and I agreed, the sweet spot number I proposed was too low to guarantee sufficient returns on their investment. So our team collectively spent hundreds of hours conducting complex costing models which, though they satisfied our investors, ultimately pushed our pricing too high. I knew in my gut that our costs were too high. I saw the weeks of work my team had put into the costing models. So I didn't put enough weight on my instincts and instead put too much on the complex models and data that underpinned the pricing we put forward.

NRStor didn't win a single bid. When I heard the results, I was furious with myself for not trusting my instincts. I should have gone with my gut. Think about it: Whether in your organization or in your life, how many times have you spent days, weeks or even months agonizing over making a decision because you were determined not to make the "wrong" choice? If you're like many people, you've likely spent way more time on "due diligence" than you care to admit. Now take a minute and look back on all the time you've spent researching your options, only to choose the option you wanted right from the start—or in my case, the option you wished you had chosen.

I'm not advocating that you become a reckless decision maker. I always sleep on major decisions, a discipline I've developed as a hedge against my aggressive nature. But when my gut speaks to me, I generally listen and more often than not my gut is right.

At Home Depot, for instance, the accepted wisdom was that the proper size for a store was 120,000 square feet. So when the home improvement chain expanded into Canada, it opened 120,000-square-foot stores. That prevailing wisdom didn't sit right with me. While a store that size might work in certain locations, I thought that, for many Canadian cities and towns, a smaller store was a better bet. After consulting my team, we decided to open new stores at sizes between 60,000 and 95,000 square feet. I didn't do any trumped-up analysis. I didn't create a complex spreadsheet. Instead, I used a combination of experience and common sense (which is, in my opinion, the definition of common sense). My conclusion: To make money, we'd need higher revenue per square foot, and we'd need to cut costs. Lowering the size of our footprint and making creative use of less space made perfect sense to us in Canada. Not so much to my bosses initially in Atlanta. We followed through with our plan anyway and found that, over-all, our smaller stores were quite profitable.

When people ask me my secret for success, I tell them this: The thing I do is that I *do*. I'm an action taker. I hire, promote and surround myself with action takers. When I look at my peers—highly successful CEOs of large organizations—I know that the best of them are all consistent action takers. There are many people who can create a brilliant rationale for choosing Option A or Option B . . . but how many make the call and begin moving? Too few. Don't allow yourself to be one of them.

## QUIT WORRYING ABOUT MAKING THE WRONG DECISION

Repeat after me: There's no such thing as a wrong decision. I'll get into the details of why later, but for now, I want you to focus on this reality. And it's a vastly different reality from anything you've likely ever been taught before. Most of us are taught, in our families and in school, to fear making mistakes. Similar to the Good/Bad blindfold, we're taught that there are good decisions and bad decisions, and that making a bad decision usually leads to failure or a crisis of some sort. Time after time, I have seen talented people stall their careers and their progress because they have been overcome by this fear.

In business, living in fear over making the wrong decision is dangerous and a waste of time. So why do so many people stall? Because they lack an alternate decision-making perspective to help them break the impasse.

When I was thirty years old, I reached just such an impasse. I was making $53,000 a year in a Crown corporation (DEVCO), which made me one of the highest-paid women in Cape Breton. I earned double what teachers made and I had a pension, both of which impressed my mother enormously. And I was bored. I'd been looking around for a new job for months, and I spoke to many senior people throughout the province about my options. No one could come close to matching what I was earning. I love money the way I love a great suit. It's thrilling to have it, but money has never been my main motivation. But I also knew that money was important currency, and I valued myself enough that I wasn't going to settle for less than I was worth. Meantime, Eric, my new husband, had completed the contract that had brought him to Cape Breton and was interested in returning to Ontario. I wanted to go. And I wanted to stay.

"Annette, what are you talking about, moving to Toronto?" said my mom, blasting me one night. "You've got it made. A great job, lots of money. You're set for life!" She was right, of course. I really was set for life. And the part of me that believed in this "set-ness" was afraid to throw away my good, secure job and move away. Complicating matters was the fact that I had no savings. ("Oh, Annette, if I could save what you spend, the money I'd have," my mother used to say. I didn't have my mother's gift for frugality. I did, however, have a convertible and the smartest-looking suits you ever saw.) But even with the sports car and good clothes and healthy salary, a part of me felt like I was suffocating. I was totally confused. Both options had pros and cons. As I weighed each choice, I found myself at an impasse, time after time.

It probably won't surprise you to hear that the tie-breaker ended up being my gut check. I checked in with the values that were most important to me. At that point in my life, freedom and opportunity were the two values I held closest. When I weighed my options against these specific values, I saw a clear winner: Toronto it was.

Once I made the decision to move to Toronto, I sprang into action. I called up every Toronto connection I had and asked them to make some introductions on my behalf. As a farm girl from Cape Breton, I knew that the best way to make a success of myself in the big city would be to become a known quantity. I went to Toronto with no job, no savings, and $16,000 in my pension account. I had a partner who was willing to support me, but as a fiercely independent woman (some might say stubborn and competitive), having to rely on his money made me feel more vulnerable rather than more secure. The legwork I did before I left Cape Breton in leveraging my network to get connections paid off. Six weeks after I hit Canada's largest city, I had a six-month contract with a federal Crown corporation. Poopie from Cape Breton had just made her first foray into the wilds of Bay Street. And she liked what she saw.

Because I love the energy and creativity of young people and try to surround myself with as many of them as possible, I have had the opportunity to mentor some wonderful emerging leaders. They will sometimes come to me facing tough decisions. The framework I offer to them—and to anyone who wants to make great decisions without wasting years trying—is simple and involves two steps. Step 1: Bet on you by aligning your decision with your core values. Step 2: Forget about making the "right" decision. Instead, focus on making your decision right by taking actions that render it successful.

In my experience, people spend an awful lot of time on Step 1 and far too little on Step 2. That is probably why so many companies go under, brilliant initiatives fail and marriages end in divorce. Step 1 isn't the problem, it's Step 2. People forget to execute their decisions. They don't realize that it's your actions that make a decision right or wrong, not the decision itself.

I spent the first semester of my freshman university year in arts. But when I met a young woman who was studying business and began chatting to her about her studies, I knew I had to switch. I also knew my parents wouldn't be supportive. So I invoked the timeless business principle of hedging my bets. I kept my decision to myself until after my first set of exams so I could see if I could actually pass my courses. At the time, many women I knew—including my sister, Dorothy—only considered traditional occupations for women, such as teaching or nursing. For someone like Dorothy, who has a brain the size of the former USSR, the memory of an elephant and unlimited amounts of patience and compassion, teaching was the right profession. For someone like me? Not so much. I knew I didn't fit the mould, yet I felt a lot of pressure to make the "right" call about which course of study I would pursue. But ultimately I coached myself to go with my gut and make my decision right through hard work. Almost four decades later, I'm proud to say I made the right call. (Dorothy thinks so, too.)

### ALIGN YOUR DECISIONS WITH YOUR CORE VALUES
Compare your options against your core values—those same values we discussed in the first chapter. If you are leading an organization or team, weigh each option against your core values, and the core values of the organization you work for. Choose the option that aligns most closely with your values.

### MAKE THE DECISION RIGHT
Step two of this framework is the most important. Once you've made the call, your next job is to make the decision *right* by executing that decision in a way that not only adheres to your values, but also makes the outcome a success. Other than the obvious exception of criminal actions, most decisions aren't inherently right or wrong. They are neutral. It's the circumstances that follow a decision—the actions taken or not taken—that make it right or wrong. You make the decision,

and then you take actions that create circumstances that support that decision. To prove this point, I'm going to turn to the world of romance. I'm as much of a romantic as the next person, but I don't believe in the concept of a preordained soulmate. You might choose to marry an absolutely wonderful person, a human being whose core values dovetail with your own. But if, after the wedding bells have rung, you immediately begin harassing said person for failing to put the toilet seat down, not being romantic enough, or not managing the household budget *exactly* as you would do it, you are taking actions that could ultimately destroy your marriage and partner into the wrong choice. I have been married twice, so you could say I have expertise on this issue. In marriage, as in life, it's the actions you take *after the decision is made* that render it right or wrong.

I met Stan Shibinsky when I was forty-eight years old. He is eighteen years older than I am. I fell in love with him immediately. He was kind, artistic and worldly, and as a successful businessman himself, he knew the requirements of a demanding career. He was The One. After five years of dating, we eloped to the Caribbean. Then we went through our first year of marriage. As mature adults who had both been living alone—in my case for more than a decade—it's fair to say we were set in our ways. For us, as for so many couples, our early years of marriage were about compromising, learning to be flexible, communicating, communicating, communicating and boatloads of forgiveness. Marriage isn't so different from business. You make the call and then you focus your energy on executing it well. It was these actions that we both took, actions that continue to this day, years after we married, that made the decision a "success." When you look at it this way, making the call is the easy part.

This concept—that you make your decisions right by adhering to your values and then executing them well—is simple but profound. That's because it takes you out of the sphere of overthinking and "would have/should have," and into the much more active realm of "what do I do now?"

Hiring and promoting people are two of the most common decisions that challenge emerging leaders. The costs of making a poor hire are large: downtime, recruiting fees, the time you spent training that employee. There's always a lot of pressure to get hiring and promoting right. In the retail world, there is a common management practice called "walking the store." Some leaders take this practice more seriously than others. At Home Depot Canada, I was as devoutly committed to walking the store as my parents were to attending Sunday mass. Being out on the floor and interacting with employees and customers was one of the best parts of my job. I met Sandra Carlucci during one of my store walks. She was a cashier and I liked her. She was friendly, bright and always curious. I invited her to walk the store with me one time and that woman asked me some great questions about my aspect of the business and gave me some excellent "in the trenches" insight from her side of the business. I saw right away that Sandra was not only likeable, she also had potential. Later, in conversation with her store manager, I pegged her as someone who could advance. She was soon promoted to become the cashier supervisor. The next logical step for her, from a career perspective, was to get into some type of store manager role. There was just one problem: she didn't have the credentials we normally asked of our store managers, many of whom had some form of business degree or training. But everybody liked her. We wanted her to succeed, and even though she didn't have the background we typically might have wanted to see for a store manager, our guts told us she would be great. So we pegged her as a potential manager and promptly began taking actions that would make the decision the "right" one. I provided mentoring whenever I could, usually on our store walks. We encouraged her to take advantage of professional development and training opportunities. For her part, Sandra executed well, learning, asking questions, raising her hand for stretch assignments, and upgrading her skills. She became an assistant store manager, then a store manager, a district manager and ultimately vice-president of a major national retail chain.

Sandra's story is a great example of the value of deciding to take a chance on someone and then following up that decision with actions that support the decision. Unfortunately, I've seen many cases where a leader decides to take a chance on a promising person, but then fails to offer any follow-up support. When the person doesn't pan out, the leader might say it wasn't a good fit. In many cases, I would suggest that it was an HR decision that wasn't well executed.

No matter what kind of call you have to make, it's how your decision aligns with your values and how you follow up your decision that renders it right or wrong. I have known this reality intuitively my whole life, but it took the single biggest threat to my career to really drive home the point.

## STAY CALM IN THE MIDST OF CRISIS

When I took the reins at Home Depot Canada, the company owned a piece of waterfront real estate in Toronto's south end. The company considered the land to be a strategic investment for potential future development. But when I stepped into the CEO position, the land was considered by the company to be vacant.

Except it wasn't vacant. The late 1990s and early 2000s were a tough period for the city's poor. With a shortage of affordable housing, some people had chosen to "move" to Home Depot Canada's land on the waterfront. Over time, as many as one hundred squatters built temporary shelters on the land. This community became known as Tent City.

Home Depot's management wasn't immediately aware of Tent City's existence. But as the population grew, it became clear that we had to take action. We began working with non-profit groups in the city in an attempt to help residents of Tent City find jobs and alternate housing. We reached out to mental health and addictions organizations, enlisting their support for those people living in Tent City who struggled with these issues. Other housing organizations began donating prefabricated houses for some of the residents. While our efforts certainly helped individuals from Tent City, the problem as a whole didn't get better. It got worse. We began getting reports of increasing drug use, violence and even sexual assaults in the settlement. To make matters worse, the land the squatters were living on was found to be contaminated with dangerous heavy metals. We approached the City and offered to pave over the land until alternate housing could be found for residents, but officials told us paving the land would require a lengthy zoning process. We could be tied up in paperwork for years. Meanwhile, public scrutiny of Tent City was on the rise.

So there I was, between a rock and a hard place. The rock: allowing people to continue living in a place they considered to be their home—knowing they would be subject to many serious health and safety risks. The hard place: evicting people who had almost nothing to their names from the place they called home. The pressure was enormous. On one hand, I had more than one hundred people who had no money and nowhere to turn. On the other hand, I had a huge health and safety threat taking place on land owned by the company I led. I had the well-being of a large group of people to consider, as well as the reputation of the company I represented. I knew that a great deal was hanging in the balance.

I had some wonderful advisors—people who specialized in working with the homeless, public affairs experts and crisis communications consultants. I consulted broadly and listened as openly as I could. Don't get me wrong. While I truly do not believe there is such a thing as a wrong decision, I don't think we should take decision making lightly, especially when people's lives hang in the balance. Seeking insight from a broad cross-section of advisors is critical. However, at the end of the day, someone has to make the call. If it's your job to make the call, you can't outsource that responsibility, no matter how great the risk you face.

## CHOOSING WHOM TO CONSULT

At some point, everyone has heard the advice about being careful who your friends are. The same can be said of choosing advisors. Do it carefully. Over my career, I have had many advisors. Some have been technical in nature. In the Tent City case, my technical advisors included the experts on homelessness, addiction, relocation and media relations. When it comes to choosing technical advisors, I always advise people to choose the best they can afford. As the head of a large corporation, I obviously had access to the very best legal and communications advice. I listened with open ears, but I always filtered any advice I received through my own internal guidance system: my gut.

The problem is that sometimes you can become so inundated with detailed information that the noise of the data starts to override that internal GPS. That's where your true advisors come in. Every leader needs a personal advisory board, a small handful of highly trusted people who share your values and can help direct you back toward your internal GPS when you've temporarily gotten lost.

For me, Frank McKenna was one such advisor. I met him shortly after I moved to Toronto, when we were both interviewed by CBC host Peter Gzowski about economic development in Atlantic Canada. He was premier of New Brunswick in those days, known as an excellent leader and advocate of all things Atlantic Canadian. He was passionate, determined and smart, with buckets of common sense. We became fast friends. After leaving public office, Frank returned to practising law and sat on a number of corporate boards, and it was at his law offices that I called him in

September 2002. He knew exactly why I had called. I didn't ask what I should do, nor did he tell me. Rather, he asked me questions that helped me work out my thoughts. And he encouraged me to trust myself. "You'll do the right thing, Annette," he told me.

Great advisors help you hear your own wisdom. Frank is one such advisor. I left the call feeling crystal clear on what I was going to do. And I remember I went to bed that night and, for the first time in weeks, actually slept through the night.

The next morning I instructed my team to begin making arrangements to evict the tenants of Tent City. We planned them to set up transition teams, composed of employment counsellors, addictions counsellors and social services. I instructed my team to ensure that all personal belongings were treated with the utmost respect, and put into climate-controlled storage until their owners—the former residents of Tent City—were able to reclaim them. We communicated with the media, our stakeholders, and the residents of Tent City. In short, we did everything we could to support our decision and make it the right one.

Some residents of Tent City went on to find independent housing and lead productive lives; others were placed in care or directed to appropriate housing. Because I was so focused on executing the decision well and communicating that decision clearly to all involved—including the media— Home Depot's reputation was not ill affected by the eviction order. And most importantly, when I look back, I know that I made a decision that reflected my values and the values of the company I worked for. Respecting people and respecting property were paramount to me and my employer—and we executed that painful decision in a way that adhered to both. Aligning my decision with my values and executing well is ultimately what made my decision the right one.

## WHAT TO DO WHEN IT'S NOT YOUR DECISION TO MAKE

Understanding the second principle around decision making—that it is within your power to make *any* decision the right one for you by taking right action—is absolutely critical to your personal and professional resilience. A career is less a sprint than a marathon. I have logged sixty-hour weeks for more than three decades. That's a lot of time over a lot of years. I have had my triumphs but I have had just as many disappointments. Having an ability to work—and lead—through disappointment has been incredibly important to my success. And the key to dealing with disappointments having to do with either your professional career, or with the company or department you are leading, is to focus on making the circumstances right through your actions. This is about understanding that you always have an ability to influence the outcome of a decision—even one that isn't yours to make.

Cultivating the ability of making decisions right through taking right action is critical not only for leading yourself, but most importantly for leading others when team initiatives fail. It's a skill I rely on to this day.

I left Home Depot Canada in 2011, after almost fifteen years with the company. I was incredibly proud of what my team and I had accomplished, but, truth be told, I'd been ready to leave for some months before I actually did. I'm a builder—I love the thrill of planting seeds and watching them grow—but maintaining an already productive field? That was never quite as exciting for me. Once Home Depot had completed its Canadian expansion and was beginning to operate as a well-oiled machine, I knew it was time to shove off into other waters. There was just one question: Which waters, exactly?

For the first time in decades, I didn't have a jam-packed schedule. I actually had time to think about what I wanted to do. And what I was really yearning for was a sabbatical. Running a large organization can be hard on your personal life. Stan had already retired from the corporate world when I met him, and had been holding down the fort, supporting me as I ran Home Depot. He was—and is—incredibly supportive of my career and the long hours it entails. So when I stepped down as CEO, I badly wanted some couple time. Stan and I decided to take a world tour. Twelve months, five continents, first class the whole way. I hadn't taken a sabbatical like that . . . ever. We hiked, swam and consumed copious amounts of insanely delicious food. And we slept. Years of working hard had left me with loads of unclaimed sleep time, and I used a lot of it during those months off. But when my eyes weren't closed, they were open. Truly open. I was travelling the world learning, rejuvenating and searching for my next big thing.

After a year and a half of travelling the world, I came to the conclusion that my next opportunity would come from one of three places: food security, water security or energy security.

Soon after we settled back in Canada, I started to visit friends and former colleagues, reconnecting and also sniffing out potential opportunities. A long-time friend and colleague, venture capitalist David Patterson of Northwater Capital, told me about a handful of companies he'd invested in that worked in the area of energy storage. We saw an opportunity to create a single company that focused on commercializing energy storage technology. We made a deal and I launched our new venture, NRStor, in 2012.

It felt absolutely fantastic to once again be an entrepreneur, at the helm of my own company. I'd gone from leading a team of tens of thousands to leading a team of fewer than ten people. As a team, we spent the next six months in start-up mode, securing financing, commercializing technology, and preparing ourselves to begin selling our technology to independent electricity system operators.

We successfully executed our first flywheel project within eighteen months of start-up. The project is operated by the Independent Electricity System Operator in Ontario and is used to provide frequency regulation for the grid. A second bidding round resulted in our submitting a number of different technologies. We felt we were competitively priced and we knew we had the best technologies out there. We felt almost certain we would be successful. Then, at the last moment, a bidding partner partnered with someone else, and ultimately won the bid. It was devastating. Totally devastating—for my team, for the company and for me personally. Between you and me, I had a little cry about it. I raged and moped for a couple of hours. Vented to some friends and colleagues. My lead investor, David Patterson, later told me that if it had happened to any other person he knew, they'd have been down and out for at least a week. I lost the better part of a morning. But by 11 A.M., years of disciplining myself to look for the silver lining and making any decision the right one started to kick in. I reflexively started asking myself how our failure to win the bid might actually be a *good* thing for our business. I pulled my team together for a debrief. Upon closer examination, we realized that we were priced too high and needed to trim our expenses. By the end of the day, we were huddled together around the boardroom table, hard at work devising a new, even bigger and more ambitious plan of action. The discussions also helped us enhance our relationships with our partners. That change of focus paid off; a few months later we were working on many new projects. The decision to award the bid to another company was not my decision to make. But by taking the right action, I was able to make it the right decision for my company and for my team.

## CULTIVATING RESILIENCE

People who know me well often comment on my positivity. If you and I were to sit down for lunch, it's probably one of the first things you'd notice. Part of that sunny disposition comes naturally—it's simply how I was made. But there's a large part of that enduring optimism that is self-made. It sounds so simple it's almost trite: look for the positive. But I've built a career—and multibillion-dollar companies—doing just that. Whether I'm making the decision, or I'm dealing with some else's decision, I look for ways to make it the right decision for me, my team and my organization.

In cases where you have the power to make the decision, you want to collect and consider the data, seek input from trusted advisors, and make a call that aligns with your values. Once the decision is made, you want to switch immediately to a focus on execution. Ask yourself what needs to happen in order to render your decision the right one.

In cases where you don't have control over a decision—and especially if things don't work out in your favour—you need to allow yourself and your team to feel the disappointment, but then you need to quickly bounce back and ask yourself what needs to happen in order to render *that* decision the right one. Is there something you can learn from the experience? Is there some way you can improve for the future? Does this "negative" decision incite you to get even more focused? Does it free you up for other, better opportunities that are more closely aligned with your goals or mission?

Most people will tell you to "find the upside." Finding the upside is too passive for me. My advice is that you *create* the upside. The more you learn to influence your own positive outcome, the more faith in yourself you will build. And when you really believe in your ability to lead well and be effective, no matter what circumstances you encounter, that's the kind of leadership strength that you, your colleagues and everyone around you can take to the bank.

## KEY CONCEPTS

1   Many talented potential leaders have stalled their progress over fear of making poor decisions.

2   There is no such thing as a "wrong" decision. Your job as a leader is to consider the information you currently have, make a decision, and then focus on ensuring the decision you made is the right one through excellent execution.

3   A new decision-making framework: Align your decision with your core values. Forget about making the "right" decision. Instead, focus on making your decision right by taking actions that render it successful.

# CHAPTER 4

# CULTIVATE A BRAZEN ATTITUDE

One thing you quickly learn growing up on the farm is that waiting for permission to do what needs to be done is a big waste of time. If a piece of equipment broke down or wasn't working right and we could see a way to fix it, we scrounged around for the parts we needed and we fixed it. Taking the time to walk the half mile from the field to the house and back again in order to explain what we were planning on doing wasted precious daylight hours.

The idea that it's better to ask for forgiveness than for permission is nothing new. Yet it surprises me how many bright young (and not so young, for that matter) leaders spend weeks, months or years waiting around for someone to give them the go-ahead to pursue a course of action that they believe to be right.

One common challenge I've noticed among team leaders and middle managers is that they often shy away from setting a bold vision for their team because they feel they don't have "permission" to do something so audacious as creating ambitious targets for their departments. In the meantime, they are sometimes surpassed by their more brazen counterparts who do find the chutzpah to take the lead, set some goals, create a vision and get working—without having to wait for the stamp of approval from their bosses.

At the heart of this obsession with permission is a fundamental misunderstanding of the nature of opportunity. In business and in life, opportunity looks less like a wide-open field than a propped-open door. If you don't jam your foot in there quickly, chances are it will close for good. People who wait around for someone else to give them permission to walk through the door often find it slammed in their faces by the time they're "ready." My advice to the people I mentor is always this: Don't hesitate when a sliver of opportunity opens up. Get yourself in there quickly. It will often feel uncomfortable. Some people may be unhappy with your moxie. But what a chance to demonstrate true leadership—if only you can learn to trust yourself and your instincts enough to get yourself into the game.

My own experience—and years of observing the best business leaders—make me think that in order to quickly move on opportunity, you don't need to be the smartest, most experienced or best-educated person in the room. All you really need is a brazen attitude. You need to be bold and a little bit shameless.

This approach may seem radical, and it is. But when you look at the direction our world is taking—from geopolitical unrest and environmental degradation to sluggish economic growth throughout the developed economies—I think it's fair to argue that the world requires the sort of leader who is willing to shake things up. The sort of person who is confident enough in her own ideas and values to stand up for them and go it alone when she needs to. The kind of leader who is brazen. If you've ever held yourself back from trying out a brilliant idea only later to see someone else try out that same idea and be a runaway success, then you know the pain of holding back. It hurts—and way more than the temporary sting of not knowing your place.

If you were born without a naturally brazen attitude (and it's my observation that four-fifths of the world fall into this group), you will need to cultivate one. The first step is to become a relentless asker.

## ASK, ASK, ASK

My first job out of university was at the Cape Breton Development Corporation, known around the island as DEVCO. It was a Crown corporation set up to create jobs and economic prosperity in Cape Breton. I started out in the industrial development arm, and within three years moved into the coal division as a long-range planner, then ultimately became assistant to the president (reporting to four presidents over two years). I succeeded by working hard, taking on jobs other people didn't want to do, and making sure my voice was heard at meetings. During those early years, I found myself on a steep learning curve. But mostly what I learned was how *not* to do things. While I had utter respect for my hard-working colleagues, I had walked into an organization that was highly dysfunctional. DEVCO was consuming federal cash to the tune of around $100 million per year. The federal minister responsible, Sinclair Stevens, was fed up with the waste and appointed a new chairman, Joe Shannon, to orchestrate a major cleanup. Joe was a barber's son from Cape Breton, and at the time owned one of the largest trucking fleets in Atlantic Canada. Joe promptly brought in a new president, along with several vice-presidents. I was doubly relieved—first because I survived the cuts, and second because it looked like change was in the air.

The disorganization and ineffectiveness that characterized the organization made my skin crawl. I was one of the more junior employees and still watching my colleagues closely as I learned the ropes of a professional working environment. However, I observed that a lot of people saw bureaucratic chaos as something that needed to be adjusted to and worked around. But I saw the dysfunction the same way I regarded a flat tire—something had to be done about it, and quickly.

Joe Shannon eventually appointed a well-established management consultant from Toronto named George Currie to the top job. George and some of his partners from the consulting firm arrived in Sydney on a warm fall day. I happened to be on a return flight from Toronto with his crew, but didn't realize it. When we landed at the airport, I made my way out to the red sports car I owned at the time, while he and his colleagues piled into the rattletrap bus that back then shuttled passengers from the Sydney airport to the hotels downtown. On my drive home, I noticed the bus broken down on the side of the road. I stopped and offered some of the gentlemen a lift—and who should accept but George Currie. It was the beginning of a wonderful working relationship.

I gave him a few days to settle into the Glace Bay offices then paid him a visit. I told him that I saw the organization was in trouble and that while I was still fairly junior, I was hard-working and wanted to help. "Mr. Currie, please give me something to do that would make a difference," I asked.

He studied me for a few moments, saying nothing. I was so excited at the prospect of finally doing something to fix the company that I too was uncharacteristically silent, holding my breath in anticipation. "Well," he said thoughtfully, "what we basically need is a complete reorganization, top to bottom."

"You got it!" I said and bounced out of the room, a huge grin plastered across my face. It would take me three days to fully grasp the enormity of what I'd volunteered to do, and about two weeks to grasp that when my new boss told me DEVCO needed a re-org, he'd been dreaming out loud . . . not giving me my next assignment. But by that time, I was committed.

For the next three months, I was a woman obsessed. I arrived at work extra-early, in order to keep up my ongoing job duties. I spent any spare time I had interviewing dozens of employees, trying to get a handle on the specifics of their jobs, how they interacted with other functions within the company, and how their current jobs prepared them for other roles in the organization. Next, I moved onto the vice-presidents who had survived the cuts, learning as much as I could about how the various arms interacted with one another, how they set targets, where the pressure points were and so on. From some corners I got lots of support, much of it grandfatherly. When I marched into the chief financial officer's office to tell him I was working on a corporate reorganization, I remember seeing a gleeful smile tugging at the corners of his mouth during our entire conversation. He answered my questions patiently and thoroughly, but I'm sure he thought I was delusional: *This girl thinks she can take on the reorganization of the entire Crown corporation?*

Many others were disbelieving and resistant. For starters, DEVCO was a man's world. I was the only woman on staff who was not an administrative assistant, and clients and colleagues usually mistook me for the coffee server during meetings. But beyond the sexism, there was an underlying resistance to change. Few of my colleagues wanted to help turn the organization around. One of the senior leaders—a guy who had been at DEVCO for years—pulled me aside. "Miss Verschuren. You don't know your place. And you better learn it quickly, young lady." His attitude was that as long as we were all getting our pensions, there was no need to shake things up . . . even if we were losing our shirts.

His comments bothered me deeply. I wondered if I was going too far out on a ledge with this ambitious new project . . . was I stepping out of line? I told him I was sorry that I had offended him and then explained what I was doing and why. I left that encounter feeling irked by his comments, a little deflated, but ultimately proud of standing up for myself. When you behave in brazen ways, you will always offend someone. I learned that the best strategy to handle people's ruffled feathers is to express regret that they feel offended, but reiterate that you feel you've done the right thing. It's a strategy I've used countless times since.

Three months after I started the project, I walked into George Currie's office with a 180-page spiral-bound report. The report included a complete overview of each of DEVCO's functional areas, a comprehensive organizational chart, job descriptions for each role within the organization, compensation recommendations, and a career path for each employee. It was, as I told him, "a cleaned-up, streamlined recommendation of what DEVCO could look like."

He opened up the report and started to go through it, shaking his head in amazement. "Annette, this would have taken a consultant six months and six hundred grand to create." One of the highlights of my recommendations was something I now know of as "cross-functionality." I knew instinctively that in order for the company to reach its potential, the engineers had to understand operations and marketing, and vice versa. Cross-functionality has become a hallmark of my leadership style and was one of the first things Currie implemented from my plan. He was blown away. And I had the distinct pleasure of having my boldness rewarded. My report had an impact and led to some positive transformations. I had positioned myself as a player in the eyes of my new boss, and by expressing my desire to help him—and asking for an opportunity to do it right away—I developed a lifelong relationship with a supportive and influential person. That's the added beauty of brazenness. While some people will hold your moxie against you, very often the people who can truly help you—senior leaders with the power and influence to see you succeed—will appreciate your boldness.

When it comes to being a relentless asker, the key is to focus on problems in your organization or career that need fixing. Are there things you find yourself complaining about? Are there clear and definite problems that need to be addressed? For example, it was clear to me that DEVCO was dysfunctional, that the layoff of senior leaders had muddled up the chain of command, and that many employees felt unclear about their career path. I highlighted this problem to my boss and asked to play a role in fixing it. And guess what? I got what I asked for.

As a very senior leader within a large company, I genuinely appreciate when my employees come to me not only identifying a problem, but also asking for the opportunity to fix it. I can't always see the problem, and I definitely value a person who is eager to take the challenge of fixing it off my back and onto theirs. So take it from me: Look for problems, pay attention to what you complain about and ask for the chance to make it better. You'll be amazed at the doors that open up for you.

## FOLLOW YOUR GUT

Another crucial aspect of cultivating a brazen attitude is learning to develop an intimate relationship with your gut instincts. When I look at, say, the financial crisis of 2008, one of the conclusions I draw is that there were hundreds if not thousands of people from the banking sector—and possibly the regulators who watched over them—who probably sensed the fishy business, but said nothing. Going against your gut is a huge mistake in business. But honouring those instincts can get you into hot water, at least in the short term.

I moved to Toronto in 1986. By then I was one of the most senior civil servants on Cape Breton Island, and had reached the upper limit of growth that was possible for me. For months I looked for a new job in Nova Scotia, but couldn't find an opportunity that fit. So I began looking further afield. By then I'd met my first husband, Eric Haites, who had a contract with DEVCO. When it was time for him to return to Toronto, I followed. George Currie made some introductions for me and within a few weeks I'd landed an excellent six-month contract that turned into a full-time job as vice-president of Canada Development Investment Corporation

(CDIC), a Crown corporation in charge of privatizing government-owned assets. My team's role was to work on the privatizations of companies the federal government identified. In some cases, like Eldorado Nuclear and Saskatchewan Mining, we worked to put two or more companies together in order to get them ready for sale. In the beginning at least, I loved the thrill of working on big deals. In my previous role at DEVCO's industrial development division, I'd worked to build small companies into large ones. In my new role, I built big companies into bigger ones and prepared them for sale.

One of the privatizations I worked on was the sale of one aircraft company to another. As part of that transaction, the government held, in a financial holding company, a number of shares of the company that was to be sold. In a political backroom, the value of those shares was negotiated to be $13 million. A few months into the job, we were approached by a major multinational company which, as part of a large acquisition, wanted to buy the airline company we held. The prospective buyer was offering $13 million. My bosses had wanted to sell off the company in question for some time and accepted the offer. As VP, I held the shares to the company, so they needed me involved in order to close the deal. They informed me of the agreed-upon price and asked me to finish up the details.

As I was doing my due diligence, I discovered that my organization had previously calculated that the value of the shares of the company we were selling was in fact closer to $20 million. This meant there was a $7 million difference between the offer and the value of the company. The way I saw it, that was $7 million of taxpayers' money that could go into schools, health care, recreation or some other good use. The offer no longer smelled right, and my instincts told me that if we settled for the lower price the decision might come back to haunt us. At the same time, I knew that the company up for sale was a strong performer, and was worth every bit of that $20 million. I voiced my concerns to some of my colleagues, but they said the price had been agreed upon in principle and that opening things up for renegotiation wasn't an option.

I disagreed vehemently. But the deal was getting down to the wire—I had only a few hours left to wrap things up. My gut simply wouldn't allow me to settle for the $13 million. I happened to be on a previously scheduled holiday in British Columbia the day the deal was supposed to close. I tried in vain to get hold of my bosses in order to discuss my position, but I had no luck reaching them. I was secretly relieved because I had already made up my mind that I could not in good faith accept an offer that low. So I decided to be bold. I called the buyer and told them the price was $20 million. Final offer. They were furious. One of their senior executives called and tried to order me to agree to $13 million. I refused. "Give me $20 million and I'll close the deal," I told them. When I hung up the phone, my hands were shaking and my neck was flaming red from anxiety. Depending on how this played out, I'd be either a heroine or unemployed.

I made my bet because I knew the buyers were under pressure—the company they were trying to buy from us was part of a much larger acquisition. Ultimately, the buyer said yes to my price and that night I was celebrating one of the biggest deals in my career to that point. The feeling soured somewhat when my bosses learned what I had done. My indirect boss wouldn't speak to me for a few days. She was initially angry at me for having gone over the heads of my superiors. Looking back I can see that it was a big, bold, audacious move. But I felt in my heart and in my gut that it was the right thing to do. I was saving taxpayers' money, which put me on solid ground, in my mind anyway.

She finally took me aside one day and told me she was proud of what I'd done, even though I'd ticked her off in doing it. She told me that if she had known what I'd been up to, she would have had to stop me. I went on to receive congratulations from various board members. One day one of the directors called me up in front of the board and said, "I want to put it on record the contribution Annette has made." Some of my colleagues were irked that I'd done such a brazen thing. But even though they were mad, they were proud. By standing up for what was right, I commanded a new respect among my peers. Despite the fact that my decision to go for the better deal could have seen me fired, within a few weeks I was promoted to executive vice-president—an opportunity I owe almost completely to my willingness to be brazen.

To be successful in business and as a leader, you have to be willing to break some rules. And the best way to break a rule is to do it in service of your gut instincts and deeply held values. Imagine for a minute that the workforce is a sea of people in grey. They follow orders, obey the rules, and subvert what makes them unique—i.e., the things they stand for—in favour of toeing the company line. Now imagine you're the person who always trusts your instincts and sticks to your values, even when you run the risk of getting in trouble for your beliefs. People like you are rare, and they stick out like a red suit in the middle of all that grey. Trust your gut and stand up for it. Wear the red suit.

## RAISE THE STAKES

Boldness is about asking for what you want, risking your reputation in order to stand up for what's right. It's also about raising the stakes. The world needs leaders who are looking for ways to play the biggest game possible, in order to elevate everyone else's play. Throughout my career, I have found that success always follows on the heels of some big, courageous action I've taken in an effort to raise the stakes, for myself and others.

A decade and a half into my professional life, I was itching for a chance to return to my entrepreneurial roots. So I set up Verschuren Ventures and began hunting around for opportunity. My research pointed out a number of promising retail opportunities, all of which I considered: arts and crafts, computers, maternity clothing and a few more. When I looked into the businesses even further, I discovered that one of the major U.S. retailers in the arts and crafts space, Michaels, had not yet expanded into Canada. Meanwhile, the market for arts and crafts supplies was large and relatively untapped.

Prior to launching Verschuren Ventures and after my time at CDIC, I joined my mentor Purdy Crawford as a VP of business development at Imasco, a conglomerate that controlled a host of companies including Canada Trust, Imperial Tobacco and Shoppers Drug Mart. During my time at Imasco, I built up a professional friendship with a man named Rick Bianchini, from Robertson Stephens, a boutique investment firm in San Francisco. I called Rick and talked to him about what I wanted to do. He invited me to a retail conference in New York. I bought my tickets that day. I remember my heart was pounding and I had that overall electric feel you get when you're about to do something big.

Three minutes after I arrived at the conference, Rick introduced me to Jack Bush, the CEO of The Michaels Arts & Crafts Stores Inc. I shook hands with him, then I told him that there was a big opportunity in the Canadian arts and crafts market, that it was underserved, and that Michaels was in a perfect position to expand into the country. I told him I'd like to invest and help lead the project.

It took a couple of minutes for him to pick his jaw off the floor, but Jack agreed to have lunch with me. Three weeks later, he took a proposal I had put together to his board. I teamed up with two colleagues, Brian McDowell and Jerry Payton, and led the expansion into Canada. We opened seventeen stores in twenty-six months. It was breathtaking. We made mistakes and we learned a ton. And it is one of the biggest accomplishments of my career.

So what does this mean for you? Success is often about creating opportunities not only for you, but also for others. Leadership isn't about playing small, it's about playing big. Had I asked the founders of Michaels if they were "interested" in the Canadian market, or if they'd be willing to "meet with me to discuss opportunities for expanding into Canada," I wouldn't have been able to capture their interest because I'd have been playing a low-stakes game. By presenting them with a concrete opportunity, and pitching myself as the woman to make it happen, I was able to elevate the entire conversation and create an irresistible opportunity for them *and* for me.

We all love people who come into our lives and kick things up a notch—people who present us with a chance to do something out of the ordinary. Don't just look for new opportunities, find ways to make them bigger. Then insert yourself in the action. When it came to landing the CEO role at Home Depot Canada, my experience bringing Michaels to Canada was one of my biggest prequalifiers. Unlike at Home Depot, no one recruited me for the Michaels opportunity. Head office for the arts and crafts company had no intention of looking north. But I kicked things up a notch for them and me and created an opportunity too good to turn down. It turned out to be one of the smartest moves of my career.

Throughout my career, I have found that the biggest opportunities for growth and brazenness happen when you adopt a "deal maker" mindset. In the stories I shared with you throughout this chapter, I adopted a series of deal-making behaviours. First, I developed an understanding of my partner's agenda. Second, I got clear on my own agenda. Third, I created a new opportunity that married both. In the Michaels case, I knew that, like most businesses, their agenda was probably growth into untapped markets. My agenda was to launch a successful national retail business. My offer to launch Michaels Canada united both agendas. Are there currently opportunities for you to unite two different agendas and then, using a dealmaker's approach, create an opportunity that didn't previously exist? While it may feel, well, *brazen* at first, over time, this approach becomes not only exciting and natural, but it can also catapult your career as a leader.

## KEY CONCEPTS

1   Leadership is about identifying and creating opportunity, and setting a bold vision. No one will give you permission to do this; you need to give yourself permission.

2   In order to quickly move on opportunity, you don't need to be the smartest, most experienced or best educated person in the room. All you really need is a brazen attitude.

3   Emerging leaders can set themselves apart by identifying problems and then taking the opportunity to fix them.

# CHAPTER 5

# MEDIOCRE STRATEGY, BRILLIANT EXECUTION

If there's one thing that will prevent you from getting results and capitalizing on your best ideas, it's waiting for the perfect plan. I'd go out on a limb and say that nothing kills progress like a brilliant strategy. When I review my career, I can honestly say that any success I have experienced has had less to do with strategic planning and almost everything to do with action. I'm not saying I don't plan, nor am I suggesting that you abandon any attempt to craft an articulate vision for your life, career or organization. Everyone needs a destination and a basic plan for reaching it. But I have observed that the main thing preventing people from reaching that desired destination is unwitting procrastination, most often in the form of the hunt for a brilliant plan.

As a leader, your job is to get results. Results aren't the by-product of thought, but of making decisions and taking action—quickly. Whether you are an entrepreneur launching a new business, a leader within an established company trying to improve operations, or the executive director of a non-profit trying to get maximum results on a shoestring budget, the ability to bring solid ideas quickly to fruition will determine your success. Anything that prevents you from deciding and acting isn't helpful.

## OPPORTUNITY KNOCKS WHEN YOU'RE NOT READY

Opportunity has its own sense of timing, and very often that timing is different from yours. After I left Imasco, I *knew* I wanted to start a retail business, and I was certain that I wanted not to launch an entirely new company, but to bring an established retailer to Canada. After researching Michaels, I approached them, and I was willing to invest my own hard-earned money in the venture. All of these moves might suggest that, when I finally signed the dotted line and became the founding president of Michaels Canada, I was totally prepared and had a plan in place for exactly how I would launch. You can see where I'm headed with this. Despite having steered myself directly into this venture, when my two partners and I signed the papers, we did not in fact didn't have a brilliant plan for how we'd launch. Life and business don't work that way. They both move quickly, so most of the time we're only able to focus a few short steps in front of us. That means that we rarely have the time to create the kind of elaborate plans we may believe we should have in place, because we are busy responding to the opportunity in front of us.

## RECOVERING FROM MEDIOCRE PLANS

Any experienced retailer with a bird's-eye view of my first six months at Michaels might have wondered if we'd still be open by the year's end. We had an established brand, an opportunity to blow open the Canadian craft market, a few hundred thousand dollars' worth of capital to build out some new stores and that was pretty much it. My entire plan for the launch of Michaels could fit on a single sheet of paper. My two partners and I knew two-thirds of what we needed to know in order to be successful: Brian McDowell and I had a strong handle on operations; Jerry Payton was experienced in purchasing. We knew very little about supply chain, couldn't afford to invest in a sophisticated inventory-tracking system or spend the time acquiring import licences, both items typically considered must-haves for a major retail operation. What's more, we were about to open a national retailer without our own warehouse. We negotiated a deal with freight company Kuehne and Nagel to rent space in their warehousing facility and pay them a fee to help us manage our inventory. It was considered a risky strategy, given how critical it was to have total inventory control. To understand why inventory control is so important, think about what it would do to a crafts retailer not to have Christmas-themed decorating supplies during the winter holiday season. Or, imagine buying twice as many wreaths and assorted Santa supplies as you need, and only discovering that you overbought in early January. You could put those Santas on sale, but by that time the market will have moved on to Valentine's Day. Either mistake could cost you your shirt. Relying on an outside party to handle such a crucial step was a risky thing to do. In fact, our "plan" had so many holes in it that if an MBA class had reviewed our start-up strategy, most would have considered us touch and go at best. Heck, I knew we didn't have a great plan. But I knew we couldn't afford to dither, wasting our time and money as we tried to come up with a better plan. We had to *act*. We had already tied up most of our capital in buying inventory, hiring a skeleton staff and building new locations. We were under the gun to open our stores and start generating cash.

So rather than second-guessing our mediocre plan, we focused our energy on ensuring we were pulling it off to the absolute best of our abilities. I made a point of developing a strong relationship with our warehouse and inventory control partners at Kuehne and Nagel, because I knew that the strength of this arrangement underpinned the success of our launch. When we saw that our first store was taking forever to open, we established a new store operator position and got John DeFranco, who was then employed by Michaels, to help us create a store launch process and then use that as a checklist to expedite the launch of our future stores. (After ten years at Home Depot, John went on to become president of PetSmart Canada.) I spent no time wondering if I should have done things differently. Rather, I focused on staying present, observing what was and wasn't working, course correcting, and making sure the actions we were taking were done as well as possible.

I'm happy to report that our mediocre (at best) strategy combined with our brilliant execution paid off. We opened seventeen stores in twenty-six months. After our initial store launch—a two-month process in all—we perfected execution so well that subsequent stores were up and running in an average of three weeks after major construction elements were in place.

## HOW WE HIDE FROM BRILLIANT EXECUTION

I believe that eighty percent of your overall efforts as a leader should be directed toward execution, toward making things happen. Only twenty percent of your time should be spent planning. Think about that: *eighty percent of your time.* In my experience, this level of commitment to execution is rare, which is why so many leaders and organizations struggle to get the results they want. I will describe some principles for executing brilliantly in a bit, but I first want to outline some of the common ways I have seen emerging leaders get bogged down by strategy at the expense of action. If you resonate with any of these examples, don't despair. Not only are these mistakes common, they usually come from the best of intentions. We overplan because we want to do a great job, and we have been taught that the way to get results is to plan well. While this "rule" might seem sensible on paper, when it comes to the real world, it just doesn't hold up.

I have fallen prey to most of these pitfalls at one point or another. As you'll discover, many seem, at first glance, to be perfectly rational things to do, when in fact they can derail progress and forward momentum. But look back on your own experience and consider instances in which your time and effort might have been best spent taking action. The key is to be aware. When you notice yourself or someone on your team hesitating or failing to take action because they are using one of these stalling techniques, gently draw attention to the problem and then refocus on your best next move.

## SEEK GREAT ADVICE

I cannot lie, I love making money and I don't apologize for
that. Driving sales and improving the bottom line of the organizations I work for has always given me a distinct sense of
pride. Watching my own personal nest egg grow has given me
similar pleasure. I am not by nature a frugal person. I drive a
nice car, I have good clothes, and my greatest pleasure in life
is taking my entire family on holidays to incredible places. But
I have always prioritized investing. From the time I started
working, I maximized my contributions to my RRSP, and as I
worked my way into more senior roles with a commensurate
rise in pay, I put even more money away. My investment money
always came out of my salary first. Everything else: car payments, mortgage, bills and fun money came out after. If you
look at graphs depicting household savings rates and household debt, you'll see (unsurprisingly) that debt levels have sky-
rocketed while savings have plummeted. For years, successive
governors of the Bank of Canada have warned that these high
household debt levels are the leading threat to our national
economy. The irony is that we have access to more financial
advisors and investment gurus than at any other time in history. There are many reasons behind the troubling reality that
underpins the financial predicament of Canadians. But one
trend I see is that people don't invest because they have *too
much* information. Should I listen to this financial expert or
that one? Should I invest in this fund or that one? What's the
very best decision I could make? And days, weeks, months,
even years pass and that person has forfeited years of com-
pound interest in favour of seeking too much counsel.

   I am fortunate in that I have access to some of the most

brilliant financial minds in the country, all of whom have their own approaches and recommendations around investing. And while I am always open to new ideas and approaches, I limit my exposure to their advice. That's because years ago, after a short period of planning, I decided how I would manage the bulk of my investments. I hired an investment advisor and together we agree on an investment strategy and what we'll put into this portfolio: growth-oriented mutual funds from respected institutions and shares of stable, well-managed companies. Do I have the most up-to-date, sophisticated investment strategy? Probably not. Do I take full advantage of the brilliant financial advisors I have within my network? I do a pulse check regularly but not so often that I might be repeatedly tempted to change my approach. Instead, I have focused my energy on trusting my own plan, one that includes input from a small handful of people, and executing this plan consistently. Sticking to this plan has allowed me to be free of second-guessing. Many years ago, I made a deal with myself that I was going to hit a certain net worth number. When I hit that number, I knew I would not have to worry about money any more. By sticking to *my* personal money strategy, a decent, though not brilliant plan that I focused on executing well, I was able to reach my number. Meanwhile, I know of others who have consistently out-earned me, but in paying too much attention to the latest brilliant fund manager or financial wizard they have not been as effective with their money.

Economists sometimes talk about the law of diminishing marginal returns. The law works like this: you eat one salted caramel ice cream, and it's bliss in your mouth. The second is amazing, but not quite bliss. The third is sugary, the fourth gives you a stomach ache. Seeking input from others is also governed by this law of diminishing marginal returns. When I am putting together a plan, or seeking input on a course of action, I will choose two or three people whom I trust, respect, *and who think differently from me.* The thinking differently part is critical. Often we consult people who think the same as a way to reinforce the path we want to take. I seek diverse input, make my decision and begin focusing immediately on pulling off that decision as well as I possibly can.

If there are instances in your life or career where you find yourself wondering what someone else would do in your situation, or constantly seeking advice and input from others, you may be using this stalling technique as a way to devise a brilliant strategy while you delay taking action. When I notice this happening in my own life, I gently remind myself about the law of diminishing marginal returns. I make sure I have heard from a small handful of people with diverse approaches, then I trust in me, make a call and act. This approach works every time.

## RETHINKING TRAINING AND EDUCATION

The smartest person I know, my sister, Dorothy, devoted her life to education and learning. She reads constantly and I have never managed to bring up a subject in conversation that she doesn't know *something* about. But even my brilliant sister would agree that it's all too easy for the pursuit of learning to interfere with the pursuit of action. Don't get me wrong, I'm a huge champion of education and learning. I'm the chancellor of a university, after all. But I have noticed that emerging leaders will sometimes opt for more training or seek more knowledge when a wiser choice might be to take a different course of action. Let's revisit my experience at DEVCO. I had gone as far as I could go in that organization. I was having trouble finding other work. I was thirty years old. What I see many people doing who find themselves in a similar situation today is earning an MBA, hoping the education will open up new doors. This is a reasonable bet. And education is always valuable. But I have to wonder whether some of those people would benefit more from taking a few of the career-propelling actions we've covered in this book: asking your network for introductions, seeking operational experience, switching sectors. Something else I see: people devoting too little time to strategic networking in favour of securing one certification after another. Again, degrees, diplomas and certifications are all wonderful, but they can also be tactics that take you away from the world of action that gets real results. If you want to get more training, by all means pursue it. But augment your training with real-world action: networking, stretch assignments and good old-fashioned hard work. These are the activities that deliver results for your team or organization. Nothing, and I mean nothing, is more saleable, promotable or valuable than your ability to take massive action and deliver results.

## DON'T WAIT FOR PERFECT CONDITIONS OR PERFECT ORDER

In a perfect world, everything happens in order. In the real world, the best you can do is to try and pull things off in approximate order. I see a lot of start-up companies led by inexperienced entrepreneurs get into trouble from over-spending because they are trying to adhere to a brilliant strategy in which everything happens in perfect order. Example: my start-up scenario at Michaels. The logical, ideal-world scenario would have been to invest right away in computerized inventory controls. After all, we had aggressive growth plans. By holding off on this investment, we knew we'd be creating headaches for ourselves later when it came time to overlay a new inventory control system on an operating retail chain. And had we been committed to doing everything in perfect order, I would have spent a good chunk of time—weeks, if not months—searching for more capital to fund our start-up. But in my mind, the search for capital in order to do things in perfect order would only hold us back from getting results. And the results we needed were sales. And in order for sales to happen, we needed some stores where people could actually buy something. If we had been focused on making the events happen in the perfect sequence, we might not have survived long enough to see our first sale.

If I ever find myself in a situation where something is taking longer than it should, I will always stop and ask myself if I'm waiting for one thing to happen in order for another thing to happen. For example, I might find myself waiting to book a meeting date with a prospective partner because we don't yet have a finalized proposal we can show him. The mistaken belief here is that we need a finalized proposal before we book a meeting. But do we? In all likelihood, no. We can book the meeting first, and finish the proposal second. This is a simple example, but it's illustrative of the many ways we slow down our progress because we're attached to things unfolding in a specific order. My rule: imperfect action is always better than order.

## TIPS ON EXECUTING BRILLIANTLY

### FOCUS ON OUTCOMES

I am your typical business operator: impatient and results-oriented. I like to get things *done*. Over the years, I have perfected a handful of principles that help me execute consistently. This in turn has helped me and the teams I work with to consistently achieve great results within our organization, no matter how awesome or average our plan happens to be.

Sometimes the pursuit of the perfect sequencing of events can prevent you from taking the actions that will deliver the results you are looking for. One way to get around this is to think about the *outcomes* you are pursuing. In the story I have just related, the *activity* of looking for more money would have gotten me an *outcome* of an inventory control system. An inventory control system is important but, for us at that time, it was not the most important outcome. The most important outcome was *sales*. With this outcome in mind, we focused instead on the most powerful action we could take that would lead to that outcome. In our case, that meant pouring our energy into opening stores: making renovations, hiring staff, stocking the shelves. By focusing on my desired outcome, I was able to take effective action. And effective action is at the heart of brilliant execution. One of the things I think we did well when setting up Michaels was that we carefully managed our resources. We delayed taking on any unnecessary overhead—like the computerized inventory control system—until we absolutely needed it. We also recognized where we were weak (in warehousing and inventory) and brought in an outside expert to help us.

Think about something you or your team is working on or, even better, struggling with. Take a moment and write down the actions you are currently taking on that particular project. Now review these actions and ask yourself this question: *Do these actions lead directly to an important outcome?* Better yet, ask yourself what are the most important outcomes you need to achieve, and then reverse engineer your actions so they lead directly to those desired outcomes. Focusing on outcomes is a core principle of effective execution.

### GET OTHERS INVOLVED

The Verschuren Centre for Sustainability in Energy and the Environment at Cape Breton University is hands down one of the most visionary, outstanding projects I have been involved with. Bringing the research centre to life required minimal planning or strategy, but a heroic amount of coordination between many groups of people.

It all got started because of a conversation I had in 2006 with the CBU's then-president, Dr. John Harker. Cape Breton was still reeling from the death of the coal industry, and we wanted to reposition the island as a centre of sustainability. A few months after we first spoke, I became chancellor of the university and we began talking in earnest about how we might strengthen the school's research and development capabilities in sustainability. So the concept of a world-class research centre was born. Bear in mind that ideas and plans for world-class facilities are hatched every day. I knew this, so did Dr. Harker. The old "brilliant planning" focus might have seen us gather some money for a feasibility study to see if such a centre would work on Cape Breton, if we'd be able to attract world-class researchers in this field, if the local community would embrace the concept and so on. We did not follow this law of brilliant planning. Rather, we switched into execution mode and promptly began circulating our vision to influential people we hoped would support us. At the time, I sat on an economic advisory committee to the federal minister of finance, the brilliant Jim Flaherty. One of my colleagues on that committee was Jim Irving, CEO of the J. D. Irving conglomerate. I called him up one day and said, "Jim, I want to build the Verschuren Centre." I shared our vision for what the centre could be: an opportunity to honour Cape Breton's coal mining past by repositioning the island as a future leader of energy sustainability. Jim lent us his support and together, we approached the premier, Darrell Dexter, to see if the province might be willing to invest as well. He saw the vision and agreed it was a worthy investment. We were able to leverage his support to secure the support of the federal government. Within the year, we had secured the necessary funding to make the vision a reality and the $31.7-million Verschuren Centre opened its doors in 2011.

I drive by the centre each time I make the thirty-minute commute from the Sydney Airport to our log house on the Bras d'Or Lake. And each time I see it I feel a tingle of possibility and a warm sense of pride at how well so many people were able to coordinate their efforts to make the Verschuren Centre a reality.

Our plan was mediocre at best and the key steps looked something like this: 1) Gauge interest by speaking to some influential people. 2) Find out what needs to be done to secure the funding we needed. 3) Write applications for funding. 4) Find a great CEO. 5) Build it. What we lacked in sophistication we made up for with our inspiring vision—a vision that others wanted to be a part of. And we executed flawlessly on another core principle: getting others involved. Your chances of pulling off big things go through the roof when you share your vision, involve others and make room for the project to be theirs as well. On the opening day of the Verschuren Centre, I looked around and saw dozens of people whose eyes were lit up with the very same pride I felt. We made it happen together.

Sometimes our very best ideas—the game-changing, status quo–disrupting concepts we have—never see the light of day because we get bogged down in trying to overplan our grandiose vision. The best way to pull off an outstanding idea, especially if it's a big idea that will require more resources than you have alone, is to seek help from people who "get" your vision, to be open to the new ideas they bring, and to share credit when the work is done.

*SMART PLANNING*

If, after reading this far, you think that I am an advocate of acting blindly, you would be wrong. But I absolutely do think that imperfect action is better than no action. And I do find that many leaders underachieve because they focus too much on strategy at the expense of execution. And I fundamentally believe there is a place for proper planning in the career of any excellent leader. In my experience, proper planning should be done at the beginning of a project, and really doesn't require more than a couple of days—a week at the most—to be done sufficiently well to begin executing.

Remember: When it comes to planning, you are going for good enough, not perfection. A great plan includes specific outcomes, a timeline for achieving them, tasks assigned to specific people and a simple method of determining if the project is on track or running behind.

In my current business, NRStor, we will have anywhere from three to eight energy storage projects on the go at once. The projects have timelines that run anywhere from eight months to a couple of years. You might think that managing multiple projects with a team of seven people would be overwhelming. We are certainly busy, but we have things under control because we plan properly and focus on executing well.

When we are first awarded a project, we will devote two or three days maximum to creating a project plan. This plan is usually encapsulated in a simple spreadsheet where we specify outcomes and deadlines, and create an overall critical path or timeline for each project. Then we address the most important aspect of planning: who is doing what. We assign each item in the project plan to a specific person.

We meet as a team each Monday morning and quickly go through every project we have on the books. Often, we will colour-code steps within the project—green means we're on target, red means we're behind. Having a simple method like "red light/green light" to help you determine within seconds if you are on track or not helps everyone execute better because it quickly highlights areas that require attention. Once we have created a project plan, we turn our full attention to working the plan, to achieving the outcomes listed on that spreadsheet. If conditions change, we will adjust our plan accordingly, but, in general, we don't second-guess our plans. We pivot at times, but we implement them.

Mastering execution skills is one of the most critical things you can do to enhance your leadership ability, provide an excellent environment for the teams you lead, make yourself more "promotable" and ensure your brilliant ideas and innovations actually see the light of day.

I have been in business for a long time. I have never seen a shortage of great ideas. What I have seen is a chronic shortage of execution skills. One of my goals in writing this book is to increase the personal potential of every reader by a meaningful amount. Imagine if you and everyone you knew were able to unlock more of your capabilities overnight. What would be possible for you and your organization? What incredible ideas and innovations would be brought out of the imaginary world and into the land of the living?

Learning how to execute well isn't hard. While you will certainly improve with time, the most important thing you need to do in order to execute well is to stop thinking and start doing. Emerging leaders will often approach me for advice. Typically they want me to tell them what I think they should do. They want help choosing between two options. I always focus on asking them powerful questions and giving them my own personal insight. But more often than not, I tell them this: If you throw enough spaghetti against the wall, something will stick. Don't waste your time and potential figuring out which piece of spaghetti is the optimal piece of spaghetti. Take off your jacket, roll up your sleeves, shove your hands into the pot and start throwing. Experiment, take chances, make mistakes. But above all, *act*. Taking massive action is the key to brilliant execution. And execution—making things happen and getting results—that's what we as leaders are here to do. Never let a brilliant plan hold you back from getting things done.

## KEY CONCEPTS

1   The main thing preventing people from reaching their goals is procrastination—most often in the form of the hunt for a brilliant plan.

2   As a leader, your job is to get results. Results aren't the by-product of thought, but of making decisions and taking action—quickly.

3   Eighty percent of your overall efforts as a leader should be directed toward execution—making things happen. Only twenty percent of your time should be spent planning.

# CHAPTER 6

# PUT YOURSELF ON THE LINE (SO YOU KNOW WHAT YOU'RE CAPABLE OF)

People rarely know what they're capable of achieving until life puts them to the test. That's why your success as a leader depends so heavily upon your ability to do just that. And while you may know that you're *supposed* to go for stretch goals, what you may not understand is just how unsettled and vulnerable you'll feel when you're really out beyond your comfort zone. In my experience, putting yourself on the line usually looks a lot like failure and rejection before it translates into success. Knowing just how challenging it will feel to put yourself on the line before you do it will make the uphill journey just a little bit easier.

## YOU'RE STRONGER THAN YOU THINK

I read an article in *Scientific American* that told an incredible story of strength under fire. Entitled "When Fear Makes Us Superhuman," by Jeff Wise (December 28, 2009), it recounted the experience of Tom Boyle, Jr., who was driving in his hometown of Tucson one evening when a Camaro abruptly pulled out in front of his car, squealing its tires and sending a shoot of red sparks onto the pavement. The Camaro hit a cyclist, crumpling the bike, trapping the rider under-neath the chassis and dragging him many yards along the pavement. Operating on instinct, Tom sprinted after the car, yelling at the driver to stop. When the car finally came to a halt, Tom could hear the cyclist moaning beneath the car, clearly in tremendous pain. Amazingly, he lifted the chassis in order to free the cyclist. The injured man, who was in agony, screamed at Tom to lift higher, and so Tom did. Eventually, the driver of the Camaro, who was by this time standing beside Tom, helped pull the cyclist free from the car Tom was single-handedly holding aloft.

At six-foot-four and 280 pounds, Tom was indeed a strong man. But the heaviest weight he'd ever deadlifted, according to the article, was seven hundred pounds. The world record for deadlifting is just over one thousand pounds. A Camaro weighs three thousand pounds, and Tom held it in the air for forty-five seconds—an incredible feat he still can't believe he achieved.

It took a tense, fear-filled moment, when a life was on the line, for Tom to uncover his true strength. Kinesiologists have found that when it comes to our muscles, we have two different types of strength. One is our "absolute" strength, the amount of force that theoretically we are able to apply. The other is our "maximal strength," the amount of force we can generate through the conscious exertion of will. Turns out there's a big gap between what we're truly capable of and what we normally do. Vladimir Zatsiorsky, a kinesiologist at Penn State University, has found that an ordinary person's maximal strength is about sixty-five percent of their absolute strength. For a trained weightlifter, that number goes up to around eighty percent.

What's really interesting to me is that maximal strength can go up under competitive or high-pressure circumstances, which is one of the reasons so many world records are broken during the Olympics—and why Tom Boyle, Jr. was capable of smashing the world deadlifting record by three times on that fateful night in Tucson.

What does this story have to do with leadership? Simply: a little bit of pressure can go a long way. When your butt is on the line and people are counting on your contribution, you learn what you're really made of. When we're comfortable and feel in control of our environment, chances are we're operating at "maximal strength." There's nothing wrong with this. But true leadership involves continuous growth. One of the things I learned fast on the farm is that if you're not growing, you're dying. There is no such thing as the status quo. When you begin to feel totally confident and in command, chances are good it's time to introduce a brand new challenge into your career, in an effort to jolt yourself into testing out your "absolute strength."

## HOW TO KNOW WHEN YOU'RE READY FOR A CHANGE

Some leaders spend big chunks of their career within the same organization. While this pattern was more common several decades ago, I still see executives today who have spent many years under the same roof. Staying with the same company has never been my preference, nor is it the approach I recommend. Exposure—whether that be to new people, novel ways of accomplishing things, or professional challenges that make your heart stop—is the lifeblood of the modern leader.

My time as CEO of Home Depot Canada was the longest tenure of my career. I absolutely loved my job—the scale of what we were trying to accomplish, the speed and audacity of our massive nationwide rollout. The adrenalin-fuelled joy of working with such smart, committed people on such an ambitious expansion plan kept me fully charged for years. But the nature of my love for the company and my work there changed as time wore on. Whereas in the beginning I practically raced into the office, toward the end of my tenure I felt so confident and in control that I was able to achieve the same impact without expending as much energy. The feeling of emotional electricity became, over time, a sensation of comfort in my role. I was happy and laid-back. And while I continued to hit my targets, I knew that laid-back is a dangerous way for a leader to be.

This feeling of being relaxed and comfortable can seem like a great thing. And for short periods throughout your career, it probably is. But staying in that headspace over the long term is dangerous. Feeling totally comfortable in your job, the sense that you've earned the right to take it easier at work, or even mild bouts of boredom and restlessness, are all signs that you may be ready to make a leap beyond the realm of what is known, predictable and comfortable. It's the only way you'll continue to grow and develop a deeper understanding of what you're truly capable of.

Understanding your limits and knowing what you're capable of is precisely the sort of self-knowledge you want to cultivate as a leader. It can help you figure out what you need to delegate, where you need outside expertise, and just how ambitious you can be when it comes to setting targets for yourself and your team. The best leaders I know have all

invested a lot of time, energy and ego into putting themselves
on the line, to challenge themselves and to know their limits.
You may be overlooking career-making opportunities to put
yourself on the line. Here are some strategies on how to do it.

## TAKE A BIG LEAP

When I worked at the Cape Breton Development Corporation, I met a man who would be instrumental in helping
to shape my career—the lawyer and business icon Purdy
Crawford. Like me, Purdy came from a modest, rural background. He was born in Five Islands, Nova Scotia and was the
son of a coal miner. From these humble roots, he went on to
graduate from Harvard with a master's degree, and ultimately
became a driving force in corporate Canada. He was incisive,
deeply intelligent, straight-talking and kind. I had a habit of
saying what was on my mind during our quarterly presenta-
tions to the board, and by speaking up I earned not only
Purdy's attention but also his respect. Purdy saw how hard I
worked and took an interest in my career. After a board meeting one afternoon, Purdy pulled me aside and encouraged me
to look him up if I ever relocated to Ontario and wanted a new
career. A few years after I moved to Toronto, I decided to take
him up on his offer.

At the time I was working for Canada Development
Investment Corporation. My boss had recently promoted me
to the executive vice-president position. It was a big job and I
was grateful to have it. But I was eager to move out of the
public sector and try my hand in the private sector. I instinctively knew that remaining pigeonholed in a single sector for
too long would limit my career options—a mistake I have

seen many people make. I was always looking around me, taking an interest in the people I admired, and dissecting their careers to see how they built their success. When I observed the leaders with the sorts of jobs and success I coveted, all of them had extensive experience in the world of business—something that told me I needed to round out my résumé with work experience outside Crown corporations.

But there was a lot to keep me right where I was. I knew that in promoting me to EVP, my boss was in fact grooming me for the CEO position. I had a big job, no doubt about it, and I felt a debt of gratitude to my employer for taking a chance on a relatively unknown woman from Cape Breton. The organization had invested heavily in me, and I had received a lot of mentoring from my bosses. But during my meeting with Purdy Crawford, he offered me a job as vice-president of corporate development for Imasco Limited, a major investment holding company. It was a tremendous opportunity—and I felt torn. I loved my job at the Crown corporation, and I could plainly see where I was headed within that organization. And that was the problem. I saw my career trajectory and knew for certain I had the skills to do the job. In other words, I knew that even if I did become CEO of the Crown corporation, I'd still be operating at my "maximal strength." I wanted to see myself at my absolute.

What Purdy was offering me was probably the biggest job held by a woman in corporate Canada during that era, the late 1980s. While I was confident in my skills, I was not certain that I had what it took to do the job at Imasco. And that's why I wanted to try it. I wanted to stretch myself and really see what I could do.

At the same time, I was nursing some feelings of guilt at the prospect of leaving. I knew my boss would be upset and I didn't want to disappoint him. And I also worried that he might take it personally, and that I'd be burning some bridges. But the desire for adventure and to test myself was greater than my fear of letting my boss down. So I took the job. As I thought, my boss was disappointed when he learned of my decision, but, ultimately, he understood.

Consistency suits some people. But if you're reading this book, chances are that you want to reach your full potential. You want to test yourself and see what you can do. I have learned that you can't test yourself and feel one hundred percent confident at the same time.

People often tell me I'm a confident person and assume that confidence has driven my career. It hasn't. The desire to push myself and test my limits has driven my career. The moment I felt fully confident and comfortable in a job was the moment I began to reassess my opportunities. If you really want to test yourself, you have to leave behind the land of what you know, and start walking in the land you don't. You have to take risks and make leaps. It's scary, exhilarating and career-making.

## LEARN TO PUT YOURSELF ON THE LINE

It was 1989, I was thirty-three years old, I had one of the tops jobs for women in Canada, and my boss was one of the greatest corporate leaders in Canadian history. I'd like to tell you that I was loving life, but that would be a lie. Work was challenging and absorbing, but it wasn't always fun. Granted, there were days when I walked to work, clad in fabulous clothes, surrounded by tall buildings and the energy of Montreal and felt a little like Mary Tyler Moore—only more senior and better paid. But life at Imasco was tough. When I first spoke to Purdy about the possibility of joining his company, I stressed that I wanted a role in operations, where I could manage people and assets. He told me that he'd find something suitable for me within a few years. My VP job was meant as a stepping stone—and it was making me unhappy for many reasons.

Shortly before my arrival, Imasco acquired a company, Genstar, which was itself a conglomerate that held a portfolio of assets, one of which was Canada Trust. Strategically speaking, Canada Trust was the asset we most prized and the reason we bought Genstar in the first place. All its other holdings were extraneous. Except for one very hypnotic fact: some of the other "assets" or companies owned by Genstar held board meetings in places like the Bahamas. For a group of Canadians stuck in freezing Montreal, winter getaways to the Caribbean were a wonderful perk

Now I adore the Caribbean, but I love pragmatism more. It made no sense to me whatsoever to hang on to a group of companies when our interests were so clearly focused on Canada Trust. The idea of holding on to an asset for the sake of board meetings on the golf course just didn't seem right. So I began bundling up the other companies and selling them off. In all, I sold $50 million worth of assets, effectively ending the board meetings down south.

Some of my colleagues no doubt saw me as a meddler, a woman who was interrupting the status quo, not to mention dispensing with luxury winter getaways. Others appreciated my decision to sell off the assets—but to preserve the peace, few backed me publicly. I had total support from Purdy Crawford in my decisions, but many of the people I worked with directly opposed my methods. I did what I thought was right, but in the end I felt completely alone.

One of the problems was that my direct boss hadn't hired me—Purdy had hired me. I wasn't my boss's choice, and I think he felt I'd been imposed upon him, which added to the alienation I felt. I learned an important lesson from that experience: When it comes to hiring people, you can't ever impose a candidate—even a star candidate—on a team. You have to get buy-in from key players before introducing someone new into the mix. Without total buy-in, that new hire will never get the support she needs to make the decisions you're paying her to make.

But aside from the interoffice difficulties, there was something else going on: I didn't enjoy the work. Despite my initial trepidations about taking on the job, within a year I'd mastered many aspects of the role. I was becoming bored. When it comes to managing your career as a leader, it's critical that you pay attention to boredom. In my experience, boredom is a sign of one of two things: it's telling you that either a) you've checked out and need to re-commit to the present, or b) it's time for a breath of fresh air.

I knew instinctively that I needed a change of scene. Thankfully, in risking the criticism of others in order to do what I thought was right, I'd helped the company but also distinguished myself. Risking criticism in order to stand up for what you believe in is a powerful way to "put yourself on the line." It's galvanizing, and the act of resolve is a powerful way to inspire others and establish your capacity to lead. With the knowledge that I had mastered my job, and distinguished myself in the process, I started looking around for the next opportunity to put myself on the line.

## ASK AND YOU SHALL RECEIVE

Another career-building technique for putting yourself on the line is to ask for advice from people you trust and admire. I am constantly amazed by the degree to which successful and influential people will share their knowledge *if you ask*. Asking for advice from senior leaders was a critical way in which I built my own leadership potential and career.

The reason that asking for help is such a powerful way to put yourself on the line is that whenever you ask for something you want, you're facing a risk: that you'll get a no. Rejection is one of our deepest fears as humans. So the most effective way to strengthen ourselves in the face of rejection is to practise the art of vulnerability by asking for what we want.

In addition, this practice is mission critical for leaders, because asking for what you want and need is a powerful way to set boundaries. As you may have already experienced, the higher you move up the organizational chart, the more "stuff" you have to deal with. Your ability to set firm boundaries with respect to time and workload will actually enhance your ability to lead effectively. And a major component of effectiveness is aligning your actions with your goals. This won't happen naturally. You have to make it happen by asking for what you need.

By the time I started working at Imasco, I knew I wanted to be a CEO. My conversations with CEOs in my circle had revealed that they all had something I lacked: operational experience. Most CEOs had had, at some point or other, responsibility for their own profit and loss statement, which showed whether they had made—or lost—a company money. While I had done hundreds of millions of dollars' worth of corporate deals at that point, I had never owned my own profit and loss statement. It was a big gap in my résumé. And it made me realize that, as lonely as I felt at Imasco, and as much as the opportunity had stretched me, I had never truly been on the line.

I reminded Purdy that he'd promised me an operational role. He pored over his companies and spotted an opportunity at the then-struggling chain of men's gift stores called Den for Men/Au Masculin. There were roughly sixty-three stores throughout Canada. Turning the chain around would be a huge challenge—one I wasn't sure I could handle. If I wasn't successful, my failure would be immediately evident in our financial statements, which is exactly what I wanted. I wanted to be responsible for my own profit and loss and to see, by the numbers, if I was truly capable of running a company.

What insight does my experience hold for you? The first is that you want to be strategic about climbing the leadership ladder. Identify the people you admire most and dissect their careers to see if you can spot patterns in terms of roles and experiences they've had that helped prepare them for their current roles. Success always leaves tangible traces, and it's your job to find those traces. Once you've identified these patterns, review your own career to see if you can check those same boxes. If not, find ways to build up the experience you need.

The second lesson is that if you dream of being CEO or running your own business, then you absolutely need to get operational experience under your belt. Finance, IT, marketing and human resources are all important staff functions, but operations is where the rubber hits the road in an organization. It's where the vision becomes reality, and where the relationships and transactions that fuel the organization actually happen. Working in operations will teach you, as it taught me, invaluable lessons about how to grow a business, deal with customers and make money. As soon as you can, find an opportunity to get into operations.

The third lesson in this story is that sometimes you have to take a step back in order to move forward. My informal research with CEOs I admired had revealed a big hole in my résumé. Filling it would require that I move down the operational chart from my current (and coveted) job. I was proud of what I'd achieved. Purdy was a legend in corporate Canada and as his vice-president of business development, I was one of the highest-profile corporate women in the country. My ego loved it, I won't lie. But the job was no longer giving me what I needed. So I booked a meeting with Purdy and we worked out a deal.

## STAYING DETACHED FROM YOUR RESULTS

I believe one of the reasons emerging leaders stay away from operational roles—even when they know such jobs are critical for the C-Suite (i.e., any role with the word "Chief" in front of it)—is that they are afraid of accountability. Being responsible for a profit and loss statement is stressful, especially when you haven't done it before. It's tempting to think that if your department or company is in the red then there must be something wrong with *you*. There are some (bad) bosses out there who may have you believe just that. But in my experience, being overly attached to your business results is no way to build a quality career.

My upbringing instilled in me the value of taking risks and testing out my ideas. Because of the way in which my parents emphasized experimentation and effort over perfection and results, I was able to pursue my goals with a spirit of freedom and improvisation, rather than being stressed over the possibility of failure. When it came to building up my career in operations, this detached-from-results approach translated well. I have seen an awful lot of business leaders literally work themselves to an early death from the stress of having to hit targets. I have also seen many colleagues confuse their own sense of self-worth with their ability to achieve their quarterly sales goals. This approach might work in the short term, but use it over the long term and you'll have no staying power.

Now don't get me wrong. When I set a personal goal—or when I involve my team and we set a company target—I do everything I can to achieve that goal. But I don't do *more* than I can. And I certainly don't equate my value as a leader with my ability to avoid failure.

Over the course of my career, I've set myself many plans and targets, some of which worked well, while others failed. The point was never to succeed one hundred percent; rather it was to get up when I faltered and rejig our plan until it *was* successful. The only way to accomplish this was to stay committed to my plan and to my success, but to also be detached from the results. This spirit has given me the inner fortitude to continue putting myself on the line. It's a skill that has given me a lot of staying power as a leader—the stamina to weather the ups and downs of business. And it's a skill I honed at Den for Men.

## EXPECT IT TO BE HARDER THAN YOU THINK

When it comes to putting yourself on the line, it's helpful to have your expectations aligned with reality. And the reality of operations is this: It's usually much harder than you think. Technically, my new role was junior to the one I'd previously held at Imasco. Purdy didn't make me take a pay cut, although I was fully expecting one. So in 1991 I cheerfully took the operating role of Den for Men, determined that I would turn the business around.

I spent the first sixty days analyzing the numbers at night and immersing myself in the business by day. It was here that I developed what would become my signature "woman of the people" leadership style. I wanted every single employee of Den for Men to know who I was, and to know that I was working for *them*. One of the ways I got to know the business was by doing "cross-functional training"—getting experience working in all the various roles at the company. I operated the cash register and greeted customers. I handled merchandising and purchasing. In this way, I was able to get a grassroots understanding of how the business *really* worked. It's tempting, as a senior leader, to assume your pre-existing management experience has prepared you to run any company. It's simply not the truth. No two companies are the same. To run an organization well, you must have hands-on experience at the front lines, at the intersection between the customer and your organization. Because without that interaction, you have nothing. Working the till, understanding merchandising— doing these various roles strengthened my relationships with my staff and customers, and also opened my eyes to specific, practical steps I could take to improve the business. Many great ideas came from our employees. We sold a lot of cigars back then. An employee suggested we bring cigar makers from Cuba to work in the store. It was a huge hit and helped to boost sales considerably.

Within a few months I had formulated a plan for revamping the business. It was big, bold and outside the box. During my travels I had fallen in love with a U.S. chain called Brookstone. The company caters primarily to travellers now, but when I took over Den for Men, it was a leading store for men's gifts. My idea was that Den for Men would partner with Brookstone to facilitate the latter's entry into Canada. At the same time, I would close some low-performing Den for Men stores and revitalize its product offerings. This strategy came directly from talking to customers and employees. With their input, I created the plan and presented it to the team at Imasco, fully expecting a rousing round of praise.

I got quite the opposite. "Nice plan, Annette, but we're not going to do that," I was told. My plan would mean that the company would need to take a "writedown"— a reduction in the estimated value of the business—which the powers-that-were at Imasco did not want to do.

Despite my best efforts at lobbying, my proposed plan with Brookstone wasn't approved. I was incredibly disappointed, but I didn't take it personally. As a leader, you'll encounter many instances in your career where the vision you've created fails to get buy-in from critical stakeholders. It's tempting to see this as a strike against you *personally*. In some cases, it will be. Had my decision to put an end to Caribbean board meetings ruffled some feathers and not been forgotten when, a year later, I pitched my turnaround plan for Den for Men? Possibly. But I simply didn't allow myself to take it personally. This was crucial, because if I had attached myself one hundred percent to the success of "my" strategy, then I would have overlooked an important fact: I'd developed a wonderful relationship with my Den for Men team, and even though this aspect of the plan wouldn't go forward, together we would come up with alternative solutions to enhance the profitability of the company. Once I realized my initial revitalization plan didn't get the support it needed, my team and I met to hash out another course of action.

Over the course of a year we streamlined the operations, cut operating costs by twenty-five percent, and despite my initial "failure" had a terrific time doing it. Up to that point, I'd never led a team of more than five people. At Den for Men I led a team of three hundred. And just as important, Den for Men gave me the operational practice I needed to test out my ideas about how companies could be run, and get the experience required to unlock some of the biggest professional opportunities of my life.

So what does this mean for you? In three words: *Get Operational Experience.* You may have the most brilliant ideas in the world. But if you can't make those ideas happen, your leadership potential will be just that—potential. In order to realize your potential, you'll need the skills to "operationalize" those plans and strategies. Operations is all about putting yourself on the line raising your hand, taking on a tough assignment and being publicly accountable for results. Take a look around you. Are there opportunities to start a new initiative, or move into an operational role where you will be managing people and assets? It may feel like a huge leap, or perhaps like a lateral career move. But learning to put yourself on the line and be accountable is the fastest way to the corner office.

## KEY CONCEPTS

1   People rarely know what they're capable of achieving until life puts them to the test. That's why your success as a leader depends so heavily upon your ability to do just that.

2   While you may know that you're *supposed* to go for stretch goals, what you may not understand is just how uncomfortable and vulnerable you'll feel when you're really out beyond your comfort zone.

3   Putting yourself on the line *may* look a lot like failure and rejection before it translates into success.

# CHAPTER 7

# EMBRACE THE P-WORD: UNDERSTAND YOUR POWER, APPLY YOUR LEVERAGE

I was a strong kid. Big muscles in my arms, thick capable hands that were more like a man's than a girl's. When I was thirteen years old, some Dutch relations came to Canada and we met up with them at an uncle's farm on Prince Edward Island. My uncle, who had been watching me work in the fields, teased me that I might be strong for a girl, but I would never be stronger than him. He was tall and broad-shouldered with a hundred pounds on me. But I was quick, fierce and more than a little indignant. I challenged him to a wrestling match. I threw myself at my uncle and had him pinned on the ground in no time. The only thing bigger than his surprise was his embarrassment. My father didn't let him live it down the rest of the trip.

If my uncle had been ready for me, I might not have been able to wrestle him to the ground. Speed and surprise were my leverage points. So I used them.

Farm life teaches you a great deal about the power of leverage because each day you're faced with tasks that are too much for a person to do unassisted. When we needed to move something heavy and didn't have access to a machine, we'd create a makeshift dolly out of rollers.

In the world of business, understanding leverage points has been invaluable to my career. Whether it has been negotiating the terms of a contract or getting myself out of sticky and potentially career-breaking situations, understanding leverage—and how to apply my power in strategic ways—has been an essential tool of both personal and organizational leadership.

As I'll explain, leverage is often dependent on timing; for example, you have more leverage at the beginning of a negotiation than once the deal is signed. But your innate strengths will always be leverage points for you. When I first started with Home Depot, I participated in an off-site training exercise the company incorporated into development programs for store and district managers. It was organized by the U.S. Air Force. We were presented with a scenario: our mission was to take over a village in a faraway country. The catch: no civilian casualties. The Air Force personnel divided us into six groups. I was chosen as leader of my team, the only woman in a leadership position in the room. It was literally one of my first days on the job, I didn't know anyone, I was leading a team in a competitive environment, all eyes were on me and I was feeling the pressure.

The whistle blew and everyone on my team looked at me for the answers. I didn't have any. But I knew I had to conquer this village and not spill a drop of imaginary blood in the process. While I had absolutely no military training to speak of, I did know my point of leverage: my ability to get people working in teams. So I huddled with my team and assigned each person to become leader of a specific section—ammunition, ground troops, tanks, supplies. Each leader came up with a strategy and we discussed them as a group. We understood who was responsible for what, we developed an overarching strategy and action plan. We pivoted a couple of times. We were quiet while the other teams were loud. One by one, the organizers, mostly Air Force pilots, wandered over to observe our team. When we finished the exercise, I was proud of my team, but felt I hadn't led them as effectively as I could have done. I didn't think we'd done very well. But it turned out we were the only team to have conquered the village with no casualties. It was a victory I attributed to my team—and to my understanding of my personal leverage points as a leader.

Unfortunately, I see many emerging leaders who misunderstand or undervalue the importance of leverage. They confuse power with manipulation and sometimes even with corruption or moral depravity. Our culture has a lot to do with that. If you were an alien visiting Earth for the very first time and decided to learn about our culture by consuming mass media (an efficient, if not enlightened way to do things), you'd probably think today's corporate world was a reiteration of Sodom and Gomorrah. Okay, I'm exaggerating, but I've observed that the words *business* and *power* when used together often have very negative connotations, which can make emerging leaders reluctant to embrace the careful use of power. The problem: the inability to use power and leverage when it's warranted can make you just like a political leader on the eve of an election—a lame duck. Lame duck leadership is bad for countries, bad for companies and bad for you. One of the biggest contributors to dissatisfaction in work teams is a leader who is so uncomfortable with conflict that she won't deal with problems. In such instances, lame duck leadership leads to plummeting morale, turnover and poor results, none of which you want happening on your watch. So let's look at leverage and power—what they are and how to use them effectively.

## UNDERSTAND LEVERAGE

Leverage is simply this: the specific point within a negotiation or situation in which you have the most power to influence the outcome. Learning to recognize these points and exert your power when you have the most leverage is critical in building win-win outcomes.

When it comes to negotiating, you typically have the most leverage before a contract is signed. The beginning of your relationship with a new employer, partner or employee is the time when you want to design the details of your alliance; it's when you want to lay out how things are going to be from that point forward. While you may understand this intellectually, I see a lot of people who underutilize their leverage, and wind up disappointed or even bitter with the deal after the fact. By then, of course, it's too late. You can't easily renegotiate a done deal. (Although at Canada Development Investment Corporation, I actually *did* renegotiate the airline deal in an effort to get more money. The difference is that I was renegotiating a deal I hadn't initially been privy to, based on the emergence of new information. In cases where new details emerge after the talks end, I think reopening negotiations is fair game.)

The trouble is that the beginning of any new business relationship is a little like a honeymoon. Everything is new and exciting, and it's easy to approach negotiations with rose-coloured glasses. You become so wrapped up in how wonderful the other party is that you might find yourself overaccommodating.

The trouble with overaccommodation is that you can make too many concessions and end up losing things that are important to you. I see this all the time. It's easy to be so thrilled that you've just landed a big job that you allow your excitement to override your ability to set boundaries and approach the new relationship from a position of true leadership. This happened to me early in my career; whatever my employers asked me to do, I'd do. I'm proud of my ever-present work ethic, but learning to set boundaries became more important for me as I advanced. Overaccommodating is common among people new to the work game. And negotiating on our own behalf is something we all need to work at if we are to secure the credibility we need to be taken seriously as leaders.

## CLAIM YOUR POWER

In late 1995, two years after my launch of Michaels Canada, I got a call from an executive recruiter. She'd been watching the Michaels roll-out closely. When I launched Michaels Canada, I was almost a solo operation, working from a desk I'd glued together myself in a back room of a Kuehne and Nagel warehouse. I had to learn to use a computer, which was a first. Twenty-six months later, we'd opened seventeen stores. I clearly had a way with large-scale retail, and people were taking notice. The recruiter told me that Home Depot was looking for a key person to lead their Canadian operations, and asked if I'd be open to discussions. I was intrigued, so I agreed to travel to Atlanta to meet the head of operations at the company's global headquarters. I immediately liked what I saw—the people and the culture. I soon realized, however, that the opportunity wasn't what I'd thought. I was initially told I was being considered for the president's position. Home Depot head office had different ideas. They wanted me to work under the existing president for a year. I had zero interest in this proposition. So I called the recruiter. "If and when they want a president, you can call me again," I said. I ended the conversation.

The truth is, I was flattered to have been selected for such a potentially plum position (even as second-in-command), but not enough to leave my current post. I loved being an entrepreneur, I enjoyed the thrill of building out the Canadian arm of the craft retailer and I had most of my personal fortune tied up in its success. I had invested a considerable amount of my own money to buy a thirteen percent stake in Michaels Canada and, according to the terms of the deal, would not be able to leave the company without relinquishing that investment at cost.

A few weeks later, my husband, Erik, and I went to Australia for a holiday. I'd been working non-stop since I launched Michaels, and was looking forward to two weeks of complete rest. A few days into my holiday, I received an urgent message from the recruiter, asking me to please reconsider my Home Depot offer. The president's job was now open, she told me. "All I'm asking is that you come down to Atlanta to meet them," she said. Maybe it was the sun; perhaps it was the fact that I was away from the day-to-day excitement of running

Michaels. Whatever it was, I was in an open frame of mind and agreed that I'd have a conversation. Then a funny thing happened. I got excited. Once you make a commitment to entertain a negotiation, your entire perspective shifts—you open up to the possibilities of what's on offer. It's an exciting place to be, but it's also an important time to remember to guard your leverage by curbing your enthusiasm, which in turn allows you to invite pursuit.

"Great!" she said. "Can you be here later this week?" Part of me wanted to cut short my trip, tell her, "Hell, yes" and jump on the next plane out of Sydney. But that same part would also have compromised my ability to safeguard my boundaries and approach the relationship from a position of leadership. Instead I said, "I'm sorry, but I'm on holiday and won't be able to make it down for a week." She was silent for a moment, but reluctantly agreed. The plain fact of the matter is that I *was* on holiday. I could certainly have cut my trip short, however, and many people would have for the opportunity to speak to one of Home Depot's co-founders. But years of observing mentors like Purdy Crawford had taught me about the dangers of appearing too eager.

## DON'T BE TOO EAGER

When you're overly eager, you compromise your power in two important ways. The first is that your desire to do the deal—whether it's an employment contract, a partnership, a joint venture or some other arrangement—overshadows protecting your boundaries. Had I agreed to cut short my Australian vacation and scurried to Atlanta for a meeting, I would have set a dangerous precedent: that my hard-earned personal time was less important than the company. I can't think of a standard more likely to create burnout. The beginning of any new venture, negotiation or arrangement is the point at which you have the most leverage with respect to setting boundaries. As the relationship progresses, the challenge switches to maintaining those boundaries—which in my case meant continuing to honour my need for personal time. As disciplined as you may be in maintaining boundaries, the best and easiest time to set them is at the outset. Don't allow your eagerness to compromise your ability to do this.

On the other hand, opportunity often presents itself not like a window thrown wide open, but more like a passing ship. If you don't catch it as it passes, that opportunity will be gone. So setting and maintaining your personal boundaries must always be balanced with seizing opportunities when they arise. Had I been, say, unemployed or in a job that made me greatly unhappy, I may well have cut short my vacation to hurry home for the Home Depot interview. In that situation, it might have been the right thing to do, because I could not afford for the ship of opportunity to sail by. As it was, I was happily employed in a dream job, so I could afford to curb my enthusiasm. Only you can decide on the right balance between maintaining your boundaries and seizing opportunity. But when I'm mentoring emerging leaders, I find it helpful to remind them that they always have the power to make a choice.

Eagerness can also make you overly attached to the out-come of a new arrangement, which in turn decreases your leverage. Throughout my career, I have found that my most successful negotiations have always happened when I was respectfully detached from the outcome. My negotiation with

Home Depot is a prime example of this. In January 1996, I flew down to Atlanta where I met with a number of senior people from the Home Depot office, including co-founder Arthur Blank.

The meeting was a big success. I liked the senior leadership, especially Arthur Blank, and could see myself taking the role that was on offer. But I wasn't convinced it was worth leaving Michaels for. Not only was Michaels my "baby," but also I had a significant chunk of personal capital tied up in the company. When I decided I was willing to take the negotiations with Home Depot further, I flagged to Larry Mercer, executive vice-president of operations, my biggest objection: the money I had locked up in an equity stake in Michaels—money I would not, by contract, get back if I walked away from the company.

"Don't worry about it, Annette," Larry told me. "We'll give you thousands of options with your contract." Now here was a point in the negotiations when I could have accepted his offer as a quid pro quo. Part of me wanted to snap up the offer, but the more experienced negotiator in me knew that this was the moment in which I had the most leverage. The company had a number of candidates to pick from—all men with more experience running big box chains than I did. I knew that I was the black sheep, but given how accommodating they had already been, I was pretty sure that they wanted me. I could choose to use that leverage to somehow make up for the cash I had put into Michaels, or I could choose not to—and walk away from the money. I chose to exercise my power.

I insisted that I couldn't walk away from what was a significant amount of money. I asked Larry Mercer how he might be able to help me sort out this objection and I left it with him. A few days later he called me back. His co-founder, Bernie Marcus, was a good friend of the Michaels owner, Sam Wyly, and he'd called Sam on my behalf. "Sam," Bernie had said, "you have someone working for you that Home Depot wants. It's a really big job and I understand there's an equity investment that she's put in. I hear she has to walk away from it if she leaves. But you tell me, does she really have to walk away from the money?" By this time, I already had an offer and a contract from Home Depot, so I felt safe knowing that, if Sam Wyly and his co-owner brother, Charles, were angry over my intended departure, I at least had a job to go to.

Sam Wyly agreed to buy back my equity investment with interest. I flew to Texas, where the Wyly brothers lived, and handed in my resignation. The brothers thanked me for my contribution and wished me well at Home Depot.

I can still remember the moment I signed the contract. It was the biggest deal of my life and I had gotten everything I'd asked for. Yes. I walked through the open door of opportunity, but I had also used my understanding of leverage to ask for everything I deserved.

Any time you are entering into a negotiation, it's a good idea to take some time to reflect on the value that you bring to the deal. Your value is your point of leverage. Next, think of all the things you'd like to get out of the deal. Get clear on the minimum you want out of the deal. Ask for the maximum up front, and be prepared to negotiate down to your "healthy minimum." Practising these behaviours will not only make you a better negotiator over time, you'll find that you also begin to create more value for yourself and others through your negotiations.

## USING LEVERAGE AS INSURANCE

In my negotiation with Home Depot, I used leverage to set and maintain my boundaries and negotiate successfully on my own behalf. By claiming and using my power (i.e., by applying leverage at the appropriate times), I was able to set the stage for a powerful working relationship based on mutual respect.

There have been times in my career, however, when I have had to use leverage as career insurance in far less favourable circumstances. As I write this, I am fifty-nine years old. I have worked in male-dominated industries for thirty-nine years. There have been many, many times in my career when I was the only woman in a sea of ambitious, aggressive, Type A, alpha males. It didn't take a magic ball to predict that, at some point or another, I would come face to face with unwanted or inappropriate advances.

I'd like to believe that times have changed and that emerging women leaders don't have to put up with the same nonsense that I did, but I'm not naïve. A few months ago, I listened to an interview of a parliamentary reporter who said that dealing with unwanted advances from powerful men was something she routinely experienced. There are of course official routes to dealing with inappropriate office behaviour. But complaints can sometimes fall on deaf ears. There are times when we have to exercise our leverage and take matters into our own hands.

A group of employees from an organization I worked for travelled to another city for a few days of meetings. We all stayed in the same hotel, dined together, and travelled to and from the meetings together. Late one evening, an organizational consultant I was working with—a superior on the organizational chart if not in moral character—knocked on my hotel door. I opened the door and asked him what he wanted. He pushed past me, slammed the door behind him and propositioned me. I was surprised, disgusted and also a little scared. I asked him, not very politely, to leave my room immediately. It took me hours to fall asleep that night. I couldn't decide if I should officially report him, or pretend that it had never happened. In the 1970s, the sad fact is that reporting such an incident was likely to have much more negative consequences for me than for him. I assumed that the man in question had had a few drinks too many at the hotel bar, and that he would be mortified by his behaviour, and I decided to pretend the entire incident had never occurred.

Flash forward two days later, when I returned to the office. A co-worker told me that the man had told him that he and I had had sexual relations. I was furious—and worried. This man was not only my senior, he was an influential person in the community and married. If the rumour continued to travel, my credibility would be badly damaged.

I was in a major quandary—I needed the story not just to stop, I needed it to be retracted. It's a sad fact that women rarely win in a he said/she said scenario. What's more, if I formally complained about the harassment, I would be bringing more unwanted attention. I put my rage aside and began to think not about what my options were, but where my leverage was. This is an important distinction. You might have several options to choose from in a tricky career situation. But when you review your options in the context of where you have the greatest leverage, you begin to see, and to claim, your power.

Because he was a man and in a more senior position, he figured that he had the greater leverage and could afford to punish me for rebuffing him. I quickly realized that I did have one point of leverage—the fact that he was a married man with children. The following morning I walked into his office, closed the door and sat down. I held up a letter.

"I wrote this letter to your wife," I told him. "It explains exactly what happened at the hotel. I will give it to her this afternoon unless you publicly retract your story." He immediately toured the office and owned up to his lie. He also apologized to me. I accepted his apology and never brought up the incident again. I still see him on rare occasions. Rather than feeling bitter toward him, I have a quiet laugh to myself and say hello. By understanding my point of leverage and exercising my power, I was able to effectively handle the situation, preserve a working relationship and move on. Justice was served, no lingering anger needed.

This story may unsettle you. You may wonder why I didn't go to HR immediately. My response is that it happened a long time ago. Chances are good that if I had formally complained, I would have lost my job. Any seasoned HR professional will tell you that if you find yourself in similar circumstances, the rule of thumb is to document, document, document. I wholeheartedly agree and would do so if I experienced this sort of behaviour today. On the other hand, still today complaints of sexual harassment go ignored, even in large organizations with clear policies such as the CBC. By all means, document. But I never advocate handing my leverage over completely to someone else.

## UNDERSTANDING POWER

There are two sources of power. One source is internal—it's your ability to own your worth, understand your leverage points and apply them. The second is external. I think of it as social capital.

Social capital is built over time. For instance, when I started work at the first job of my career, as an economic developer at DEVCO, I was leader in title only. In the beginning, people only listened to me because of my job title. People below me technically had to listen to me. By working hard, building relationships and winning trust, I was able to influence people because they trusted me. At a certain point in a leader's career, people will listen to you because of what you represent to them. Several years after I took the helm at Home Depot, I had created a strong base of support among our twenty-eight thousand employees. Each and every time I visited a location, I toured the shop floor and engaged with as many employees as I could. Over time, I developed a reputation as a leader who truly listened. The resulting trust in turn boosted my power and credibility as a leader.

My ability to foster a team environment was instrumental in driving the overall performance of the company. Thus, my performance and track record became another source of strength. In the next chapter I will give you some strategies to help you build stronger relationships. But for now, understand that when it comes to influencing outcomes, inspiring others and making genuine change, your social capital is truly the source of any "power" you might have. Had the twenty-eight thousand employees at Home Depot not respected me, there's no way I could have spearheaded such a successful expansion. People simply would not have bought into my vision.

## USE IT OR LOSE IT

Power is like a muscle—if you don't use it, you lose it. Or perhaps better put, you lose touch with it. When you have built up your skills and social capital to such an extent that you can, say, run a big company and lead thousands of people, it can be easy to lose touch with reality. Or, as my brothers would say, to have a head so big you can't fit through a door. A big head is the quickest way to lose social capital. Watch carefully and you'll notice that an egomaniac's power comes not from the amount of respect he has earned, but from the fear he elicits. I have watched many upstanding people become literally drunk with power. It's human nature. When you are leading a large organization, you're surrounded by many people who simply want to please you. If that's not a recipe for a big head, I'm not sure what is.

The antidote to egocentricity is humility. And the best way to cultivate humility is to serve. It's also a great way to build your social capital. I sit on a number of major corporate boards. I also sit on the foundation board of the Centre for Addiction and Mental Health, one of the world's leading hospitals and research centres. I serve on that board because of a deep personal commitment I have to mental wellness. And I sit on the board as my way of giving back to my sister, Dorothy. She has been my biggest supporter, and a lifelong source of inspiration. She was the smart sister—I could never ask her about a topic she didn't have at least a working knowledge of. She was always there to listen to my ideas, celebrate my wins and bear witness to my setbacks. She battled depression for a period during her life, and after she pulled through it I vowed to support causes that champion mental health as much as I can.

My career has given me the opportunity to build connections with many wealthy and influential people. These relationships—my network, if you will—are a huge source of my social capital. I could let that social capital languish, or I could put it to good use and exercise my power. I choose the latter. As a member of the CAMH Foundation, I connect the organization's fundraising head with people who have significant means and are passionate about mental wellness. I love using my "power" in this way. Not only does my social capital become a force for good, but I also derive huge personal satisfaction from using the resources at my disposal to create good in the world.

It's never too early to begin building your social capital—and your power—by using it. I'm not just talking about volunteering for the office bottle drive. I'm talking about taking a supply-and-demand approach: connecting people who can help each other, making introductions. I suggest adopting this habit: Each time you meet someone new, ask yourself how you can help that person. And then help them. The beauty of social capital is that it's self-reinforcing. The more you spread it around, the more you have to give.

If you want to lead, sooner or later you'll have to learn how to use power. If you're the type of person for whom the word *power* has unpleasant connotations, it's useful to think about power not as a tool for control, but as an influence for good, a tool you can use to advance your larger mission.

## KEY CONCEPTS

1   Whether you are negotiating the terms of a contract or getting yourself out of sticky and potentially career-breaking situations, understanding leverage—and how to apply your power in strategic ways—is an essential tool of both personal and organizational leadership.

2   Leverage is the specific point within a negotiation or situation in which you have the most power to influence the outcome. Learning to recognize these points and exert your power when you have the most leverage is critical in building win-win outcomes.

3   When it comes to negotiating, you typically have the most leverage before a contract is signed.

# CHAPTER 8

# YOU ARE MORE THAN YOU

The biggest and hardest personal transformation you will need to make to be a great leader is shifting from accomplishing things all on your own to achieving things through other people. Leadership is a team sport—you can't do it alone. The problem is that so many of us start out as sole practitioners. We're first hired because of our technical competencies. But over time, and especially as you move into senior leadership roles, technical competency has less and less to do with effectiveness.

When you were first hired, chances are that you had a clearly defined set of tasks that you were paid to accomplish. Sure, you may have needed to interact with other people to complete those jobs, but your personal tool box of skills and capabilities was sufficient to get the job done. If you were to review your career path, you'd soon see that with each successive promotion or, if you're an entrepreneur, growth stage, the skills in your tool box shrank in relation to the demands of the job.

When I first worked at DEVCO in the industrial development division, I had the skills I needed to do my job. I sat down with business owners, reviewed their financial statements, learned the ins and outs of their business, helped them identify opportunities to grow and made the necessary introductions to set them on the right course. While I sought out mentors and advisors with specific skill sets in an effort to keep learning, I could accomplish the vast majority of my job description by calling on my own resources.

Today my tool box is much bigger than it was thirty-nine years ago. But even when I take all my skills and experiences into consideration, my own skill set and resources are enough to accomplish less than ten percent of what I'm responsible for achieving as chair and CEO of NRStor. The same was true when I led Home Depot. In both cases I didn't have all the tools I needed to accomplish my objectives—not even close. Yet in both cases I was more than equal to the challenge. Why? Because of a simple but profound principle of leadership: you are more than you.

So how is it possible to be *more* than you? As I've mentioned, the goals you are working to accomplish take far more resources than you personally have within your tool kit. Therefore, you must work through people in order to achieve that specific vision. This is not to say that technical competency isn't important—it's crucial. But a leader's technical competence plays less and less of a role in a company's success as he or she takes on greater levels of responsibility. Your team's efforts become your efforts, and their ability to accomplish their goals becomes the lead measure you use to determine whether your overarching vision will, in the end, be accomplished. If I want to know whether a particular energy storage installation is going to be successful, I don't look only at what I'm doing; I look at what my team and partners are doing. Their success is predictive of the company's success, and of my own effectiveness as a leader.

The fuel that keeps this virtuous circle going is relationships. Surrounding every great leader is a web of interconnected relationships that hold her up. Nurturing and supporting relationships with your colleagues, stakeholders, family and friends is a critical habit. Ignore or damage your relationships and you put both your career potential and the success of your organization in jeopardy.

My ability to build relationships with people inside and outside my team was one of the big reasons Arthur Blank bet on me to lead Home Depot Canada. I was up against a host of men with far more experience than I had. But the leaders of the organization had seen the effect that a leader's poor relationship-building skills can have on a company's performance. As you read in the Introduction, the man I replaced at Home Depot Canada had a massive office and an exclusive parking spot. These were common executive perks, but contributed to difficulties in getting his team aligned and earning the confidence of the parent company. Without a strong and committed network of support, he couldn't successfully meet the ambitious Canadian roll-out plans that had been set before him. He did go on to great success in other settings.

I'm amazed at how many emerging leaders devote huge chunks of time to developing their technical skills, and far too little time to building up their interpersonal skills. I'm incisive with a financial statement and know my way around a spreadsheet. But I got to where I am today not because of my financial wizardry but because of my ability to inspire, build trust with and motivate other people. If you were to talk to the business people that know me best, they will usually rank relationship and connection skills as my most important competencies. Some of it comes naturally; I'm an extrovert born into a big family. But the skills that come naturally to me—building trust, connecting people, and staying positive—were rough diamonds when I started out. Diligent practice has improved them. Here are some habits that will help you develop top-notch relationship skills, tools that will help you lead not only a successful company, but also a more fulfilling life.

## INVOLVE PEOPLE

I don't really believe that you can motivate another person. Motivation is deeply personal. It has to come from *you*. When I first moved to Toronto, the sight of so many skyscrapers all in one place thrilled me. I remember stopping on the sidewalk on my way home from work one day, looking all around me and telling myself, "One day I'm going to *own* this city." I'd probably phrase it differently today, but the point is that I wanted to reach the very top. I wasn't sure what that would look like exactly, but I knew it meant doing my best and being my best. As mentioned, Purdy Crawford called it the "fire in the belly," and he considered it a crucial characteristic in the people he hired. He knew that a deeply rooted desire to hit the big leagues was important for success in business, and he knew it wasn't something anyone could give to someone else. It had to come from within. I agree completely. For me, the big leagues was "owning the city"—which in turn meant reaching the pinnacle of Canadian business. For you the big leagues might look very different. But no matter what the "top" looks like to you, there's only one person who can truly motivate you to get there—you.

Even though psychologists tell us that motivation is intrinsic, there's still a lot of talk among leaders about the importance of motivating our employees. What we mean isn't making them want to achieve a goal they don't truly want to achieve. When I talk about motivation, what I'm really talking about is creating an environment where people have the support they need to reach the goals and ambitions they have laid out for themselves. I have found that no matter how incredible people's work ethic, their desire to work hard and do well is so much higher when they have played a role in setting their own targets and creating their own work plans.

I learned this on the farm. Every one of us kids was a "good worker." After my father's heart attack, we simply had to contribute. But even as a child, I noticed that there were two different kinds of farm work. First, there was the work we had to do on a daily basis: feeding the animals, milking the cows and cleaning the stalls. Second, there was the work we didn't technically *have* to do, but could *choose* to do— repairing a section of fence, cleaning the milk tanks, clearing land. I always found that I was more excited by and proud of the jobs that I took upon myself—much more so than the milking, which simply had to be done. When I had a choice about what job I took on, I took more pride in the work and felt happier when I'd finished it. On the other hand, when I finished the "have to do" chores, what I usually felt was a mix of exhaustion and sweet relief.

I also grew up in a household where kids were actively involved in making decisions. While my parents had the final say in any new farm initiative, they always discussed the issues around the dinner table and consulted us. When it was time to buy a new piece of farm equipment, we were invited to sit at the kitchen table as my parents presented the loan officers with their plans. They believed we kids needed to hear their vision. When the farm loan board turned down my father's application for capital to invest in equipment that would allow him to siphon liquid manure from the barns and spread it on the fields—a more common practice today, but unheard of back then—we as a family had many group discussions about how to make it happen without the financing. This was in the 1960s, when the overriding belief about children was that they should be seen and not heard. My parents weren't trying to be ahead of their time, although they were innovating in agricultural sustainability; they were just being practical. From the age of eight, all of us spent hours a week working on the farm; we handled a lot of important chores and had an important perspective. Making decisions about the farm without consulting us would have been irresponsible; it would have been poor leadership.

I have brought this practice from our farm in North Sydney, Cape Breton, into my work in corporate Canada. As CEO, I know I always have the final call on major decisions and have overall responsibility for setting the direction of the organization. But I don't create that vision alone. I involve my team in determining in what direction our company should move. As a group, we usually have far better ideas together than any single person could have alone, which is why it's so crucial to make a practice of involving the people around you in decisions.

I have found that involving others is especially critical during challenging times—and this can be one of the most difficult times to do it. When Home Depot Canada was first expanding into British Columbia, we had a heck of a time. The stores were not as successful as we wanted them to be because we didn't have the right mix of products, and overall we just weren't performing well. Arthur Blank pulled me into a meeting and told me that if I didn't turn things around, he might appoint the team from the northwest United States to run the provincial business. This was not news that I wanted to hear. It stung and there was a part of me that wanted to "take care of it" on my own—I didn't want my team to doubt me or my abilities. But as a leader, ego can be a liability. A lifetime of experience collaborating in tricky situations had taught me that the best solutions came from groups of people. I brought in my senior team and told them about Arthur's suggestion. They were motivated to keep the business—none of us wanted to lose B.C. to our American counterparts. Together, we came up with a merchandising and operations plan that turned the market around in a year. We improved "assortments," or product mixes, expanded certain departments, and upgraded management teams, all of which helped us boost profitability.

We had a similar experience in Quebec. We first entered that market with the notion that Quebec was simply another Canadian province, where people happened to speak French. We didn't appreciate the true uniqueness of the market, and we fumbled in our early years. I consulted with my team and together we decided that we clearly needed a different merchandising strategy. They devised a marketing strategy that was unique to the Quebec market—different from anything that was being done in the U.S. and other parts of Canada. It was a much bigger investment as well. I listened to my team, convinced the senior leadership in Atlanta that this was the way to go, and within a short time was celebrating our Quebec success together with my team.

Today at NRStor, my entire team pulls together on a weekly basis to review our strategy and opportunities. We're operating in technology that is driving change in the energy market—we need to be nimble. I simply could not see the opportunities on my own. Every major business success has always been the result of a team effort.

Learning to involve your team in helping to set the direction for your department or organization does more than ensure they stay motivated. It saves *you* time and frustration. A colleague recently shared with me a story about "Elizabeth," a division leader for a national engineering company. Like many new leaders, she'd been promoted because she had excellent technical skills, and found herself in charge of twenty people, with very little leadership training to speak of. Within a few weeks, she had a to-do list that was beyond her capacity. She began doling out defined tasks to her employees and this gave her some breathing space. But within a few weeks, she found herself drowning in work again—and this time she didn't even feel she had enough hours in the day to call people into her office and delegate specific tasks. "I just wish they'd be proactive and think of ways to help me and take stuff off my plate!" she confided to one of her mentors. What she failed to understand was this: it's hard to be proactive when you don't know where you're headed. Elizabeth hadn't involved any of her key employees in determining targets or a vision for the office. Because they didn't know where the business was headed, it was difficult for them to identify areas where they could help. They simply didn't have enough information. By not involving her team early or often enough, Elizabeth unwittingly violated the principle that makes leadership actually work. Rather than leveraging relationships to amplify her individual efforts, a failure to involve others and delegate ate into her time, interrupted her leadership focus and actually rendered her less effective.

It's a good practice to hold quarterly or annual planning meetings with your team where together you can set goals or targets for the future. Once the team goals have been set, get individuals to set smaller goals that fit into your overall objectives. Once you've identified these individual targets or goals, allow each person on the team to contribute ideas about the most important activities they can take on that would help them achieve the overall target. Then meet monthly to check in on everyone's progress. It sounds simple, but this practice requires a lot of discipline to maintain. But you'll find, as I have, that when people have a say over what they're building and how they go about achieving their goals, they approach the work with far more energy and motivation. They "own" it.

## DON'T HOG THE PUCK

Once you've involved your team in setting a direction and delegated the work, your next job is to recognize their progress and achievements. Involve, delegate, recognize—these are the three critical steps for working *through* other people so that you can be more than you. It's amazing how the simple rule of giving credit where credit is due can be so hard for some people to follow. If you choose to hog the puck—and the credit—your reputation may take a short-term flight, but your long-term results and legacy will speak for themselves.

Take Lee Iacocca, the legendary CEO of Chrysler. When he first took the reins of the company in the mid-1970s, it was close to going out of business. Chrysler had lost millions on a series of recalls. He set to work transforming the company by hiring great people, introducing new models of vehicles and petitioning the U.S. government for bailout loans. His strategies worked and he rescued the company from the brink of bankruptcy.

But the golden years didn't last long. Some years later, the company got into financial trouble again. But this time, rather than focus on a team effort—putting the right people in the right places and investing in improvements that would keep the company competitive over the long term—Iacocca may have focused his attention largely on preserving his legacy and reputation. In the view of some of his biographers, he failed to approve successful new designs, designs the troubled company badly needed, because he worried the credit for their success would go to members of his team—not to him. Ironically, he tarnished what would have otherwise been a hugely impressive legacy.

At Home Depot, I travelled once per quarter to various stores, where I presented teams of employees with awards and recognized sales performance contest winners. Each quarter I'd hold two-hour meetings with my store support team, updating them on how we were doing, and how our performance was measuring up against the strategy. At each of those meetings, I'd recognize leaders whose contributions were especially significant. We also had a program where associates could nominate their peers for their work and initiative—an important way to get a team thinking about the importance of taking ownership for team performance. The bottom line: one of the keys that drove Home Depot Canada from $660 million in sales to $6 billion under my tenure was our team culture. When I won Retailer of the Year at the Retail Council in 2005, I brought my entire team on stage with me. I didn't win that award—we did.

The key takeaway is to look for opportunities to thank people and give them credit. As a leader, your team's success *is* your success. If your team or company does well, that's a reflection of your leadership, and you will often be the person in the spotlight receiving that recognition. Never hesitate to give the people whose hard work has enabled you to be in the spotlight the credit they deserve. When people weren't doing well, I'd always take them aside and tell them privately exactly what they needed to work on in order to improve, and we'd then meet monthly to monitor progress.

## PRAISE THE RIGHT THING

When I was sick in hospital as a teenager, my dad gave me a piece of praise that I have treasured my entire life. "Annette," he said, "you are my best worker. Now don't tell your sister and brothers." (I haven't ever told my brothers he said that, and I'm trusting that you won't either. But I bet he told all of my siblings they were the best too.) I choked up right away—I was filled with pride. But I was also filled with another powerful feeling: determination.

In 2006, world-renowned Stanford University psychologist Dr. Carol Dweck published a landmark book, *Mindset: The New*

*Psychology of Success*, that explores the psychology of praise and success. Dweck's research showed that when it comes to offering praise, there's a right way to do it, and a wrong way to do it. The right way, argues Dweck, is to praise *effort*. The wrong way to is in exchange for *results*. The reason: we always have control over our efforts, but we rarely have control over results. When you praise something a person has no control over, Dweck's research suggests, you create an environment that promotes a "fixed" mindset—a culture or belief system that suggests intelligence or ability is static. Dweck argues that people or organizations that adopt a fixed mindset create a culture where people try to look "smart," which in turn leads to avoiding challenges, getting defensive, lacking perseverance, underestimating the importance of effort, or feeling threatened by the success of others—all of which tend to result in stalled progress. This is particularly troubling for leaders because our success depends on the individual ability of the people we lead to keep on growing and achieving. If they stall, we stall.

On the other hand, when you praise effort, you encourage what Dweck calls a "growth" mindset, which believes that intelligence and ability can be developed. This in turn leads to a desire to learn, which translates into a tendency to embrace challenges, persist in overcoming obstacles, understand the value of effort, take the lesson from criticism and find inspiration in the success of others—all of which lead to ever greater levels of achievement.

One of the perks of being a highly visible leader is that you can use your position as a way to acknowledge others for their efforts. When walking the Home Depot stores, I gave out badges and publicly thanked employees for handling tough customer service complaints or for consistently doing a great job in merchandising or operations. While I linked these efforts to the larger sales targets, what I acknowledged was hard work and effort. This acknowledgment was inspiring to the employees and to me as well.

Does this mean that you shouldn't celebrate when, say, someone in your organization lands a big piece of business? Of course not—in fact, you should look for as many reasons to celebrate success as possible. But rather than congratulate for winning the business, congratulate for the hard work, effort and dedication it took to land the business. The more you make praising effort over results a personal practice, the more you will infect those around you with a wonderful affliction: the desire to put in their best effort, whether they "win" or not.

## MEAN SOMETHING

As you have probably gathered by now, my childhood spent on the farm is central to who I am and how I operate in the world. I refer to the farm in conversation at least a few times a week. Talk to anyone who knows me, and they'll be able to tell you at least one story about my experiences on the farm: my father's heart attack and how it forced us to come together and run the entire operation, the dirt under my fingernails, the smell of cow manure that simply would not wash off in the shower, the kind neighbour who used his vacation time to help us put in the hay.

In the beginning of my career, my tendency to tell stories about the farm was accidental; a situation would emerge and I'd be reminded of something that happened in my life on the farm. But as I developed as a leader, I began noticing some interesting things. I discovered that when I launched into a story about the farm, the person I was speaking with would relax a little. His eyes might soften, he might smile more. And after I'd shared something about myself, that person was likely to be a little nicer to me, or, at the very least, more cooperative.

Our brains are hard-wired for narrative. People remember information better when it's presented in story form. Also, stories elicit a powerful emotional reaction in listeners. What's more, when you share personal stories in work settings, you force yourself to be vulnerable. And when you make yourself vulnerable, you open up a space for someone to fill with empathy. Finally, personal stories tend to have a powerful, universal quality. Your father may not have had a heart attack when you were ten years old. You may not have ever experienced the agony of someone teasing you because you smelled like cow shit. But when you hear these stories of mine, I'm willing to bet you find yourself moved by them. Maybe you connect with the values that come through so clearly when I tell my stories: the values of family, resilience, forgiveness.

We live in a confusing, uncertain world. We're experiencing a time of rapid change that is possibly unprecedented in human history. Whether you want it or not, in this context, your role as a leader is probably more profound than you realize. What your people want from you is encouragement and support, but also meaning. They want you—and what you say—to *mean* something. And the best way to mean something is to tell your story.

Because I have been so forthright about sharing my farm stories at work, my personal brand now reflects my core values, values that are embedded in these stories. People know more about me than my résumé. They know where I come from, that I value family above all else and that I'm not afraid of working hard. Their knowing these details about me has helped to forge stronger relationships and connections with colleagues and employees.

I'm not advising that you begin sharing the intimate details of your life at next week's Monday morning board meeting. I do, however, recommend that you find ways to work more of "you" into your communication with colleagues and clients. Consider a few stories that either epitomize or shape the values you hold most dear and consider sharing them when the time is right. Take your greatest successes and share them, offering some carefully picked details, as a way to demonstrate your passion and vision to investors. Use story as a way to connect with and inspire people. It's an incredibly effective tool for building your personal brand, your impact, and the depth of your relationships.

Lately I have been doing more and more speaking engagements. The parts of my speeches that people connect with and remember are always the tales from my childhood, my experiences on the farm and how they shaped me.

## DON'T FIGHT OTHER PEOPLE'S BATTLES

It's an unfortunate aspect of human nature that many of us want someone to carry our burdens for us. And when you step into a leadership role, you quickly realize that the perks of the title can quickly get worn down by the weight of the burdens that your subordinates unwittingly lay on you.

Some time ago, I heard a story about Glen, a recently promoted senior leader in a mid-size manufacturing company.

His office gave him a great view of the parking lot. And it also gave him a front-row seat on a trend that many new leaders face: he never had enough time to get work done, but the people who reported to him often had too little to do. So there he sat at his computer watching his employees arrive in the mornings—he'd taken to arriving early in order to catch up on work. And there he'd sit in the evening, watching his employees leave, while he stayed on to—you guessed it— catch up on work.

Glen was a good man, a hard worker, and he was described by his staff as a caring boss. But he was committing one of the top errors I see new leaders commit—an error that hurts their relationships with the people they manage, destroys their work-life balance, and cuts their chances of ever being more than they are. The error, to paraphrase business consultant William Oncken, Jr., was that he couldn't quit putting "monkeys" on his back.

Let me explain. Several times a day, employees came into Glen's office with problems they needed solved. These problems ran the gamut from staff conflicts and scheduling issues to inventory problems and contract negotiations. The problems were monkeys on the backs of his staff; they didn't have the solutions, so they brought the monkeys to their boss. And Glen took them on, at first happily, then grudgingly, until he was so overwhelmed and overworked that he began to resent his employees when they left at the end of the day, usually a few hours before he called it quits.

What Glen didn't realize was that he was actually creating the problem by taking the monkey off his employee's back, and putting it onto his own. I sympathize with his experience completely. As a young manager, I did my share of monkey-adoptions. When I was at DEVCO and a team I was on was given an assignment, I'd usually do most of the research and then write the report. I did this a lot. It helped me get recognized, but it soon became an expectation. Everyone wanted me on their task team because I happily collected the monkeys. Near the end of my time there, I realized that until I got myself into a bigger leadership role where I could reset the expectations, this trend would continue. My dream was to run the railway and coal preparation plant. I wasn't successful in my bid, so I had to move on.

I soon learned that there are an inexhaustible supply of monkeys. You simply can't deal with them all. At some point or another, you need to learn how to put them back where they came from: into your team's hands.

Today when my staff come to me with a monkey, I usually offer a variation of this response. I ask if they have conferred with their colleagues. If they have, then I'll do my best to hear their question as soon as possible. If not, I ask them to first discuss the problem with their colleagues and then set a time to meet with me once they've come up with a solution to the problem. This really works—it stops silly, incidental problems from jamming up my day, teaches my team members to keep their own monkeys and helps me evaluate the staff who have the hardest time working with their colleagues.

I never jump to handle their problem, or answer their question without first inviting them to find another means—preferably a means that doesn't involve asking me to handle it. To quote Dr. Phil, we teach people how to treat us. If I accept all the monkeys from my staff, I've trained them to believe that I'm the person who handles the monkeys. If I gently hand the monkey back to them, then I'm training them to understand that they are every bit as talented at handling monkeys as I am. The bottom line: You can't effectively lead a team or yourself if you are drowning in other people's problems. Resist the urge to do other people's thinking for them—even if it feels like the quickest route. Empower others to solve their own problems. This will give them the skills they need to be successful, set the appropriate boundaries in your relationship, and allow you to get back to the important work of being a leader.

I have always been transparent with my team. When there's a problem identified in their reviews, we agree about the areas where development is needed and then put a plan in place around it. There's no greater happiness to me than seeing employees become better leaders. I see it, their colleagues see it, their customers see it and, most importantly, they see it themselves.

## KEY CONCEPTS

1 The biggest and hardest personal transformation you will need to make in order to be a great leader is shifting from accomplishing things all on your own to achieving things through other people.

2 Involve, delegate, recognize—these are the three critical steps for working through other people so that you can be more than you.

3 No matter how incredible people's work ethic is, their desire to work hard and do well is so much higher when they have played a role in setting their own targets and creating their own work plans.

4 Praise effort, not only results.

# CHAPTER 9

# YOUR NETWORK IS YOUR NET WORTH

You may have brilliant ideas and a powerful natural leadership style. But without a strong network of supporters, you'll never have the impact you need to create change and become the leader you are meant to be. In order to bring your talents and skills to bear, you'll need a web of people to support you.

I'm living proof that anyone can build a powerful network. I come from about as far away from the Old Boys' Club as you can get. My parents were immigrants who spoke broken English, and I didn't leave Cape Breton until I was thirty. Yet today my network includes some of the world's most powerful and influential people.

If you've been following the career moves I've described so far, you've probably detected a pattern: all of the opportunities I've been presented with have happened because of someone I knew. For example, the chance to pitch the Canadian expansion of Michaels came about because I called a former client and told him about my plans to get into business on my own, which prompted him to introduce me to the company's CEO.

My first summer job was at Sobey's, a grocery store, in North Sydney. I worked as a meat packer. It wasn't a bad-paying job, but I learned through our neighbours, the Caldwells, that

CN Marine had very good-paying jobs. My sister, Dorothy, worked at the local five-and-dime and at a small restaurant and made hardly any money. I learned through her experiences what *not* to do. Mr. Caldwell, who was the father of my friend Peggy Caldwell, was very much in the know, so one day I asked if there were any opportunities at CN Marine. I told him I could work the night shift any time during the week or on weekends. He said, "Leave it with me, Annette." A few weeks later he called to say there was a foreman's clerk opening on the night shift. I would have to work with the yardmaster of the railway to plan to put the rail cars on the rail-car ferries between North Sydney and Port aux Basques, in southwestern Newfoundland. I told him I was qualified to do it. I was just sixteen years old. I didn't have a clue but I had a great attitude and I learned from some great people who worked with me. To this day my boss Gord MacLeod and his wife, Lois, are dear friends. Gord showed me the ropes and helped me work with captains of the boats and the yardmaster to make sure I balanced the loads carefully so there would be no problems with the crossing. That job financed my way through university and I graduated debt free. I always had a horseshoe up my—*oops*, in my purse.

In my experience, most emerging leaders know *in theory* that networking is a career maker. But they don't make networking enough of a priority. The reason? I think it's because they are operating under the mistaken belief that success and effective leadership are all about *what* you know. That couldn't be further from the truth. Effectiveness as a leader is all about *who* you know.

If you want to use your unique ideas, insights and strength to lead organizations, earn the recognition you deserve, and create genuine change and innovation, you will need to learn how to expand your influence through your network.

## YOUR BELIEFS SHAPE YOUR REALITY

No matter how strongly I encourage people to network, I have found that they always feel uncomfortable if they don't change their beliefs around what networking actually means. In a networking study published in *Administrative Science Quarterly*, researchers from the University of Toronto, Harvard and Northwestern University discovered that the idea of networking can "smell" so bad to some people that it makes them feel physically dirty. In the study, people were asked to recall past networking experiences, or to imagine themselves in a networking scenario. Then they were given a set of word-related tasks, including word completion exercises, or choosing adjectives from a list of options to describe their experience. The researchers found that the subjects associated strategic professional networking with the need for cleaning supplies, or even with words like *dirty*, presumably because they found something morally distasteful about the very idea.

Interestingly, research subjects that had higher levels of power—for instance, senior lawyers versus junior lawyers—didn't have the same level of "dirty" connotations around networking. This study essentially underscores my own observations of networking: powerful people understand and even enjoy it, while up-and-comers neither care for it, nor do it. The irony? It's the up-and-comers who truly *need* to network.

These findings concern me for two reasons. The first is that, by failing to network, you are robbing yourself of the opportunity to make the connections you need to bring your ideas to life. The second is that the corporate world needs to change—we need to create and innovate in order to forge the environmental and social change our world so badly needs. For instance, research from the Washington Center for Equitable Growth suggests that the top 0.1 percent of American households have a share of wealth equal to that held by the bottom ninety percent. That's a level of inequality not seen since the Great Depression. And it's a level of inequality that does not serve society well.

So what does inequality have to do with networking? If the only people who enjoy networking are the people who already have power, then all we're doing is reinforcing existing power structures. Our world needs us—and you—to disrupt those power structures. And professional networking is an important way to do that. Trust me, if my own networking could take me from the shit-covered stalls of a remote dairy farm to the upper echelons of the corporate world, think how it could transform the opportunities available to you.

## YOU CAN BE CALCULATING AND KIND

One of the conclusions the researchers drew from the networking study is that thoughts of "moral impurity" lead to feelings of physical dirtiness. Many of the people who said networking made them feel dirty felt that way because, deep down, they believed there was something morally wrong with networking. That raises the question: How can you make networking feel right?

I believe the answer is in the approach. And my approach to networking is very, very simple: Give, give, ask. One of the values my parents drilled into my siblings and me was the importance of helpfulness. In our family, being told you were "useful" was one of the highest compliments. To paraphrase the great Canadian philosopher Red Green, "If you can't be handsome, you can at least be handy." For as long as I can remember, I have approached all my new relationships with a spirit of helpfulness. This goes back to my years in a two-room schoolhouse when, from the age of five and straight on through to when I left for middle school, I was the teacher's helper. To this day, whenever I meet a new person, I look for how I might be able to help that person get what he or she wants.

Approaching networking with the goal of providing help will settle your moral compass and erase any feelings of "dirtiness" you might have. But helpfulness is only a part of my approach. Remember, it's give, give, ask. You need to give twice as much to your newfound relationships as you expect to get in return. So I might look for opportunities to help new acquaintances a few times before I contact them with a specific request for help. Adopting this approach ensures I'm adding true value to my network. As an added bonus, by giving as much as you can, you'll find that over time you have a strong group of supporters who are eager to return the favour.

A common mistake I see emerging leaders make is that they believe the fact they're junior means they don't have help to offer a more senior person. That's usually not the case. Let's say you meet a leader at an event and she tells you her company is struggling to recruit new employees; perhaps you can offer to send some qualified candidates her way. People usually look for opportunities to trade favours. All you have to do is accept their offer of help. For some of you, that will be the hardest part of all.

## ACCEPT HELP

You probably know someone who just will not accept help. They won't ask you to refer clients or put in a good word, nor will they let you pay for dinner or hold a door. I am as independent as they come, but seeing people who won't accept help drives me nuts because it violates an important law of human connection: We're all in this together. To cultivate the influence you need to ensure your ideas are heard, you need to not only offer your help to other people, but also accept help. When you offer help but don't accept it in return, you create a power imbalance within your relationships that breaks them down, rather than builds them up. Asking for help necessarily makes you vulnerable, which deepens your relationships with people in your network.

When I launched Michaels, I knew very little about the logistics of retail: shipping, storage, just-in-time inventory and so on. These are areas of business where it's critical to have a detailed understanding to remain profitable. I shared my challenge with the gentleman who leased us warehousing space. Turns out, he was an expert in this area. He gave me excellent advice, and ultimately we subcontracted some of these services to him. A few years later, when I started at Home Depot, I was again in need of help navigating a totally new and challenging business environment. I approached the other presidents in the company and asked them to teach me the business. They accepted and went on to teach me a great deal and to be incredible supporters of my work within Home Depot. They are supporters and friends to this day.

Very often, I see emerging leaders working hard to help others and not asking for help themselves. Both approaches are wrong. When it comes to networking, you need to help twice as much as you ask for help, but you *do* need to ask for help. I think of the process like a big game of balloons. You know: that simple game you played as a kid, where you and a friend tapped a balloon back and forth, and the object of the game was simply to keep the balloon in the air. Each time someone accepts help, it's like the tap that keeps the balloon in the air. You can't allow your partner to do all the tapping. It's no fun that way—she's playing the game while you're just standing there watching. Don't stand and watch. Ask for help.

One way to ensure you ask for help is to think about what you need. Perhaps you need introductions, advice, support, resources—these are all things about which you can ask for help from your network. I never go into a meeting without knowing exactly what I want to get out of it. I take the same approach at networking events. I recently used a speaking engagement as an opportunity to test out some new ideas I have around leadership. My goal for the event was not only to meet some new people, but also to get feedback from three people on the ideas I was sharing. And because I was clear on what I wanted, I was able to get it. Just as you think of ways you can assist a new person you meet, think about things you might ask that person to help *you* with.

## NETWORKING IS A LONG-HAUL GAME

Did you ever plant a garden? You sow the seeds in May and after months of watering and careful weeding, you harvest the vegetables in September. Like seeds, relationships need time and TLC before they are ready to bear fruit. One of the reasons I've seen some of my protégées try to give up on networking (I say "try" because I never actually let them give up on it) is because they aren't getting immediate returns on their investment of time. Would you ask someone you'd just met to drive you to a doctor's appointment? No. In the same fashion, you can't expect instant referrals from new professional relationships. You need to invest time and effort before the relationship bears tangible fruit.

My career is chock full of relationships that I have carefully nurtured over the years, that have ultimately rewarded me in many ways. This might sound cold and calculated to you, but I assure you it's not. I build relationships with people because I genuinely respect and admire them and value their friendship. I want to help them be successful, and know that I cannot be successful on my own—no matter how much I have achieved.

## PUT IT IN YOUR CALENDAR

As I will share in a later chapter on staying organized, I live and die by my calendar. If I want to make sure something happens, I have to put it in the calendar. I encourage emerging leaders to book time for networking, especially if it's not something you enjoy, or you don't have to do it as a regular part of your job. Look for interesting events to attend and make a habit of attending them twice a month. When you are at the events, don't spend the entire time with one person. Spend ten minutes with each person and learn as much as you can about that person—what they do, what's important to them and so on. Then, follow up one to two days later with the people you felt aligned with, and invite them out for a coffee, or schedule a brief phone call. Make a habit of having one of these "connection meetings" once per month. By attending events, you are exposing yourself to new people and environments. By following up with key people you met at the event, you are deepening your relationships with some of the people in your network. This simple, one-two punch approach to the mechanics of networking is straightforward and effective.

For some people, walking into a room filled with people they don't know can be intimidating. That discomfort can be felt by even the most consummate networkers—present company included. Whenever I'm in a new situation where I don't know anyone and I feel my nerves start to jangle, I remind myself to focus on "give, give, ask." I'm at that event to help others and make a difference in the lives of people who really need me. The first order of action is to figure out who those people are. Taking this approach puts me into a service mindset, and that goes a long way toward reducing the low-level anxiety that's part of any new social situation.

## EVALUATE YOUR NETWORKING

As I have climbed the corporate ladder, I have discovered that I have to balance my innate desire to help everyone with the reality that my most important resource, my time, is also my most limited. My schedule fills up twelve months in advance. And while I would like to attend all the events, dinners, meetings and informal gatherings to which I'm invited, it's physically impossible. (As you may have guessed, I'm far beyond the two events per month quota I recommend you start with.)

The same will happen for you, if it hasn't already. So the question becomes, how do you evaluate your network to ensure you're not only adding value to the relationships, but also getting the support that you need to advance? Here are some strategies to help.

### *DOES EVERYONE PUT SKIN IN THE GAME?*

When you say the word *networking*, some people conjure up an image of a guy in an ill-fitting suit throwing out business cards like confetti. Unfortunately, that stereotype exists for a reason. You don't have to have been in the game for very long to have spent way too many hours at low-quality events, or groups where the majority are there to hustle sales, and the connections you make are superficial at best. One important metric you can use to evaluate your network is how "connective" it is. Are people within your network introducing you to other people? Are they asking you for introductions and adding tremendous value to the people to whom you introduce them? Too often "networking groups" are glorified chat rooms. There's lots of griping and general discussion, but not much in the way of solid, practical help. The practical value of your network is directly tied to how much skin its members are willing to put in the game. Talk is wonderful, but it's also cheap. If your network doesn't do a good job of connecting people, or offering tangible help, then you need to cultivate relationships with like-minded people who will actually help you.

Another important consideration in evaluating your network is the quality of information it provides. The specific type of information you need will depend on what your ultimate aims are, but there are three main categories of "informants" most people require from their network: technical, practical and social.

### TECHNICAL INFORMANTS

In my situation, I know that I need specific sets of skills and expertise related to my business. The energy storage industry is highly technical and constantly evolving. To stay ahead of the curve, I need to be regularly connecting with scientists, engineers and other techie types who have a strong handle on where the science and technology of energy storage is headed so that we as a company can be responsive, prepared and innovative. My recommendation is that you too look for opportunities to develop relationships with technical informants in your industry, be they thought leaders, academics or others who have mastery in your field. Let's say you are a senior manager in an economic development non-profit. You would want to count economic development researchers, professors and possibly even authors among your network. Having these types of people in your network keeps you current, cutting edge and relevant.

The chief technology officers of companies I work with in the energy storage industry help me understand the why and how of how electrons work on the grid. Today I surround myself with smart people with great experience. For me it is very simple: I know what I can't do. Early on at NRStor I hired people that complemented me. Yes, I have the experience of running companies, but if you have the wrong mix of people you lose. I also have discovered that it's better that they don't have to be like me. I want them to have good values, but I like it when they challenge and give me a different perspective. I have a young team around me today. VP Jason Rioux has enormous experience in the electricity market and brings a wealth of project management and operational experience to the team. Jennifer Manning is our lawyer and brings great experience in corporate law and infrastructure development. Alexander McIsaac, manager of business development and projects, is a sponge for new knowledge and a great financial modeller, and is learning so much about this industry. And the list goes on.

### PRACTICAL INFORMANTS

Practical informants are the people who can help you make progress and get things done because they know the lay of the land. Again, just who these people are will depend upon what you do and your goals, but the key is that they are able to offer practical ideas and aid that will take you closer to your goals— if not the entire way. You will probably want to have practical informants in categories related to money, law and government. So if you're an entrepreneur, you want to have people in your network who are in the government departments related to your field. In my case, I'm operating a business that works within a highly regulated industry. Government policies play a huge role in my business, so I need to have relationships with people in the energy branches of both the provincial and federal governments so that I'm staying abreast of new initiatives or changing regulations.

Anyone working in business, whether you're an entrepreneur or a leader within a for-profit organization, should have relationships with banks and funding agencies. These relationships are critical should you require financing to fund your next big idea or, in a worst case scenario, money to float the business if you encounter a crisis. Strong relationships with lawyers are invaluable as well. In some cases, practical informants may simply be mentors who have already accomplished the same goals. Their experience can cut years off your learning curve.

I often try to grab a coffee with a practical informant, who could be from business, government or my family. I sit down with a clear problem I want to solve and toss ideas around with them, which helps me move toward a solution. Whether it's one of my siblings, or business colleagues Frank McKenna, Elyse Allan (CEO of GE Canada), Linda Hasenfratz (CEO of auto parts company Linamar), my board colleagues, or David Patterson, I always recognize people that help me, and say thank you. Whether it's by a call-out in public, a private handwritten card or a thank you to a partner or child, people want to be recognized, even those that say they don't. It costs so little to do.

### SOCIAL INFORMANTS

While the majority of your network will be made up of technical and practical informants, it's also very useful to have a few of what I call "social informants" within your web of relationships. Social informants are the kings and queens of homecoming, the presidents of student council. These are genuine, influential and highly likeable people who are incredibly well connected and can make introductions on your behalf that you could never make on your own. Purdy Crawford was one such person in my network. I had tremendous respect and admiration for him, and made an effort to connect with him in the moments before or after board meetings because, trust me, the wisdom that man could throw out in a few words is more than most people manage to share in a lifetime. He ultimately became a life-long sponsor and friend, made key introductions for me and, as the stories I've already shared underscore, he had a tremendous influence upon my career trajectory. Without his support, it would have taken me longer to get where I am today.

When I look around at most of the high-powered business people I know, all have enjoyed the help of "social informants"—part sponsor, part friend—and these powerful connectors open the doors of opportunity. The key to working with social informants is that you honour the help they provide you with help of your own. When Purdy asked me for favours, I always pulled out the stops to make them happen.

## DO YOU HAVE THE RIGHT MIX?

In addition to evaluating your network for the *types* of people it contains, you also want to ensure you have the right mix of networking activities. In a 2007 article for the *Harvard Business Review*, Herminia Ibarra and Mark Lee Hunter, who teach at INSEAD, a world-leading graduate school of business, identified three distinct types of networking, all of which are critical for your career: operational networking, personal networking and strategic networking. When I read the article, I laughed because I had intuitively been engaging in all three types of networking for my entire career.

*OPERATIONAL NETWORKING*

The objective of operational networking is to develop strong working relationships *within* your team so that everyone can get their work done well and efficiently. This is the most common type of networking because it's the easiest to do and the returns are immediately obvious. One of my most important professional relationships is with my associate, Allison Blunt. She manages my calendar, guards the gates so that I can focus on strategic priorities, and filters the communications and requests that come my way so that I don't have to spend my days responding to emails. Nurturing a strong relationship with Allison is crucially important to doing my job efficiently. Similarly, I have to invest in developing relationships with other people on my team—other colleagues and staff, investors, suppliers and partners.

You probably know that operational networking is important, although you might not have called that relationship building you do with your colleagues "operational networking." Ibarra and Hunter found that most managers have major blind spots when it comes to cultivating relationships. The problem: they don't have a broad enough definition for *team*.

During my days at the Home Depot I was constantly innovating. How do we build sales, and improve productivity and the customer service experience? I was always so impressed when I challenged our teams. I remember our first Mow Down Pollution event. We worked with local utility companies, lawn mower manufacturers, and the consultancy Summerhill Sustainability Programs. The idea was to replace greenhouse gas–emitting gas-fired lawn mowers with electric and battery-operated mowers. This was when the greenhouse gas problem was just beginning to gain attention. The first year of the program we got about one hundred people to bring in their old lawn mowers and get a $75 credit against an electric, battery or push mower. By a few years later over eight thousand mowers were being exchanged.

During those years I headed up the Environmental Council for Home Depot, where we did amazing work to improve forest management practices around the world by choosing to buy from companies with better practices and that had third-party certification. But not everyone liked what we were doing. I remember John DeFranco and Gino DiGioacchino, two of our great merchants, presenting what we thought was the wildly successful Mow Down Pollution program, and the response was mute if not deafening in its silence. I spoke to one of my colleagues afterwards and wondered why. He said, "Annette, here greenhouse gases are not something that is top of mind—you could lose sales of higher-value products by taking this approach." Could I have done a better job of communicating and getting operational support from my peers? I would say probably yes. Our sales were exceptional and if I had led with sales and the added benefit of reducing greenhouse gases, I wonder if I could have influenced more of my peers. The Canadian team presented many operational procedures to the U.S. company as our best practices and many were adopted. It was how we operationally networked with them that was important.

I learned this lesson the hard way. In 2004, the company invited me to run the Home Depot Expo Design Center—a higher-end version of the regular stores. The business was in trouble. I put together a ninety-day plan to attempt to turn around the company. As always, my plan was based on heavy consultation with staff and customers. One of my key recommendations was to immediately close twelve Expo Design Center stores in order to boost profits. My team members and many of my peers all supported me. But my plan was quickly shut down when I presented it to the senior leadership team. The problem: I hadn't done my homework and built solid relationships with all of them. Nor had I taken the time to discuss my plan with them one by one. If I had done these things, I would have learned that shutting down stores was something alien to Home Depot's culture. Such an idea needed a much more patient approach. Three years later, as it turned out, the company asked me to close twenty stores. I felt frustrated, mostly with myself. Had I done a better job of building relationships at the outset, my cost-cutting plan probably would have worked. But a few years later, the weakness of the housing market caused the company to close all stores.

### PERSONAL NETWORKING

Many time-starved up-and-comers laugh at the idea of "personal networking" because it implies they actually have personal time. I get it. Nothing comes without a cost, and perhaps the biggest sacrifice I have made to build my career is my personal time. The irony is that I enjoy my work so immensely that it never feels like a massive sacrifice. But there are certainly times I would rather be kayaking around Bras d'Or Lake than reading financial statements in preparation for a board meeting. That said, making time for personal networking is extremely important.

Professional networking can sometimes feel very high-pressure: your boss or colleagues may be observing you, a deal may be on the line. People often hold back from practising new social skills in high-pressure situations such as awards events or post-AGM networking receptions. That's where personal networking comes into play: it provides a great opportunity to build your social skills, increase your knowledge beyond your technical and work-related skills, and find much-needed support. And the best part is that engaging in personal networking will often enrich your professional relationships as well. Unlike operational networking, where the focus is on building relations *internally*, Ibarra and Hunter point out that when it comes to personal networking, the focus is on building relationships *externally*.

For some time I have sat on the foundation board of the Centre for Addiction and Mental Health (CAMH), where I've developed a close working relationship with Darrell Gregersen, president of the CAMH Foundation. One of the fundraising strategies I encouraged the foundation to focus on was securing large donations from wealthy patrons whose values aligned with those of the foundation. I took careful stock of my own network, made some introductions, and accompanied Darrell to her meetings with these individuals. Ultimately, some of them decided to offer generous donations. Being a part of the team that made that happen felt amazing—certainly it enhanced my relationships with my fellow board members, but it also strengthened my bond with the people who donated. Suddenly we had a profound shared experience and common language, completely outside the world of work. When we run into each other at corporate events, there is a closeness and spirit of partnership that wasn't there before. Such is the power of personal networking.

I encourage the emerging leaders within my team to do the same. I recently encouraged Alexander McIsaac, my NRStor associate, to join a volunteer board of a non-profit. There were three main reasons I suggested he volunteer his time. First, I firmly believe in the power of volunteerism and the duty we all have to give back. Second, I believe that serving on a non-profit or charity board can give emerging leaders solid governance skills. And third, this is a young man who devoted himself to his work—I wanted to ensure that he was finding opportunities to broaden his interests and knowledge. The organization he was helping to govern went on a major fundraising drive a few months after he joined. Not only did he help to raise money for a great cause, he broadened his network in the process.

### STRATEGIC NETWORKING

As my relationship with David Patterson illustrates, when you are engaged in "strategic networking," you are planting relational seeds that may one day transform into giant oak trees.

The purpose of strategic networks is to create leverage, and link resources within your organization to powerful organizations outside. One of the most profound linkages I ever made was with none other than the president of the United States.

It was late winter in 2006 and I was in Cancun, but I wasn't on holiday. The prime minister had invited me and five other business leaders to present our views on enhancing the competitiveness of North American companies to the leaders of the three NAFTA countries—Stephen Harper, George W. Bush and Vicente Fox.

I spoke about several issues, but the most important was the softwood lumber dispute—a major trade problem that had a huge impact on Home Depot's Canadian business. The Canadian and the U.S. governments and their respective lumber industries disagreed about Canadian lumber exports to the States. The Americans believed that because so much of Canadian softwood came from Crown land, it was being unfairly subsidized by the federal and provincial governments. Therefore, they applied heavy import duties, which raised lumber prices, and in the mind of the Canadian lumber industry unfairly hurt its competitiveness.

After I had finished my presentation in Cancun, President Bush came over to me to ask me some questions. It was the first time I had met him, and I can tell you that, politics aside, I liked him. While he was not my favourite president, he was a warm, kind and charming presence. "Mr. President, this is one of the most significant trade disputes of our time," I said. "It's been going on for too long, and I feel you need to get personally involved in addressing it."

My heart was thumping so loudly, I was worried he might hear it. I wasn't sure how he'd take my attempt at telling him what to do—I was sure it didn't adhere to any protocol for dealing with leaders of state. But I also saw that conversation and his willingness to engage with me on the issue as an opportunity to influence an outcome that would have a significant impact on the health of my business.

The president listened carefully and when I finished talking, he said, "I'll look into it." People close to Bush later told me that when he landed back in Washington, he spoke to some of his aides who were charged with handling the dispute. "There's a woman who runs Home Depot Canada who was at the meeting," he apparently said. "She says we need to get this resolved."

A few weeks later, in April, Canada and the United States reached a landmark agreement on softwood lumber. While there were a great many people working on this issue for a long time, I like to think I had a small part to play in resolving it.

The effect on Home Depot's business was immediate. The prolonged tariffs on Canadian softwood lumber had raised prices for consumers in the U.S. and forced our sister company, Home Depot USA, to cut back on its Canadian purchases. Rather than sourcing wood from North America, the company had begun to source it from northern Europe. Resolving the softwood lumber dispute made Home Depot more cost competitive, which benefited not only our customers, but also our bottom line. What makes my experience with George W. Bush a great example of strategic networking is that I was able to forge a connection *outside* my company and link that relationship *inside* the company. This is networking at its most powerful, influential and exciting.

So how do *you* network strategically? Volunteer for new projects or initiatives that are happening within your organization. Join industry associations and aim to get involved at a high level. Research trends in your industry and attend conferences and events in that area. The thing about most strategic networking relationships is that they rarely have any obvious "payoffs" today, because they are so future oriented. Take the Wayne Gretzky approach to networking. He famously advised aspiring hockey stars to "skate to where the puck is going." I encourage you to network where your career and organization are going. It will help you more than you can imagine.

## KEY CONCEPTS

1   Without a strong network of supporters, you can't have the impact and speed you need to create change and become the leader you are meant to be.

2   A big part of your effectiveness as a leader is the relationships you develop.

3   The approach to networking is very, very simple: Give, give, ask.

# CHAPTER 10

# GO FAR TOGETHER

In 2005, nine years after taking the reins at Home Depot, the Retail Council of Canada named me their Distinguished Retailer of the Year, reflecting Home Depot's rapid and successful Canadian expansion. Like many leaders, I am competitive and goal-oriented, and I love to win—but never alone. When I took the stage to accept the award, I was flanked by a group of employees, and I accepted the award on behalf of all Home Depot Canada's employees. The gesture wasn't a display of false modesty. It pointed to the truth: that any success the company experienced had nothing to do with my efforts as an individual, but everything to do with our work as a team.

Retraining yourself to think, work and achieve as a team is one of the most profound, effective and career-making shifts you will make as a leader. This goes beyond simply delegating: it's about consciously looking for ways to enhance the team dynamic, and to support everyone on the team to unleash their full potential. People pay lip service to the importance of teamwork all the time and everywhere. But walking the teamwork talk is much rarer. There are two main reasons for this: the first has to do with speed, the second with heart. When you look at who gets promoted into leadership positions, you'll find a lot of "doers"—people who stand out for their ability to achieve results quickly and effectively. But what initially made them successful, their personal effectiveness, can trap emerging leaders and stall their progress. I call this the "I'll do it myself" problem.

You were promoted because you are a top performer. According to researchers Michael C. Mankins, Alan Bird and James Root, of the global management consulting firm Bain & Company, top performers are roughly four times as productive as average performers. Because of this, many emerging leaders make the mistake of taking on the extra work because they think they can do it faster. (These same people often wonder why they are the last to leave at night.) This desire to go fast and save time ultimately means you rob your team of opportunities to contribute, unwittingly crush motivation and work longer hours than you need to because you are doing everyone else's job.

The second reason that so many people pay lip service to teamwork without actually supporting it, is that to really lead a team and make everyone on that team *better*, a leader must wade into the interpersonal fray. You need to become a mediator in human relations and human potential. This is one of the most challenging aspects of leadership: it requires patience, empathy and a willingness to be vulnerable. And for many of the Type As who drive themselves into leadership positions, this kind of human or emotional "messiness" is, well, pretty scary.

And this is precisely why leadership is about bringing more of *you* to the table. The higher you rise, the more you must depend on others. Depending on people makes you vulnerable. But if you truly want to lead, you'll have to embrace the reality that leadership is a team sport. I find that the antidote to the discomfort of feeling vulnerable is remembering why I'm doing it in the first place: because I know I'll go much further as a part of a team. I also remind myself that leading people is a privilege. Once you achieve the goal of ascending into a leadership role and become, say, an executive director or vice-president, that goal switches to a responsibility. Now you are responsible for leading people, facilitating their work with colleagues, and ensuring they are able to bring the very best of themselves to their work.

## THE GREATNESS OF TEAMS

Most of my early notable achievements were the result of work I did alone, the complete overhaul of the organizational structure at DEVCO is one example. Today, nothing I accomplish is related to my solo efforts—*nothing*. Even my health, the asset I prize more highly than money or prestige, is the result of a team effort: my husband, Stan, cooks incredible meals, my trainer keeps me in top condition, my coach helps me master my psychology, my physician helps me monitor any medical conditions that might flare up. Behind any great accomplishment, there is always a team of committed, hard-working people. And when these players are working in an atmosphere that focuses on bringing top talent together under the umbrella of true collaboration, it's astounding what can be accomplished. According to a 2013 article on star teams in the *Harvard Business Review*, it took six hundred Apple engineers less than two years to develop and deploy the company's disruptive new operating system,

OS X. Meanwhile, a similar-scale project at another tech giant required ten thousand engineers and more than five years. The lesson: Great people working together in high-functioning teams drive massive results.

If you're reading this book, it's probably because you want to make an impact in this world, and you want to make real change. Most of the leaders I know feel this calling. Because results are so closely tied to a high-performance team, learning the skills you need to foster, support and leading a collaborative team will be critical to your success. On one level, you probably know this. But if you're like many emerging leaders, you have lots of room for improvement when it comes to leading a team of people. I have seen many would-be leaders stall their careers out of a failure to effectively lead a team. And you know what stopped them? A desire to move quickly—and a corresponding inability to bring the team along for the ride.

## GO FAR, GO TOGETHER

One of my favourite leadership quotes is this African proverb: "If you want to go fast, go alone. If you want to go far, go together." I am a huge fan of individual initiative—but never at the expense of teamwork. I'd go so far as to say that my most painful business mistakes have come about because I, like so many emerging leaders, was impatient and believed I saw a chance to move faster on my own.

Great leaders accept responsibility for their decisions and accountability for what happens on their watch. The buck stops with them. And that's pretty much the only time as a leader that you should go it alone. I learned this the hard way, when I pitched a new idea at a quarterly meeting without doing any prior consultation with my team. Here's a quick tip that could boost your ability to bring your most disruptive and innovative ideas to fruition: the worst way to bring up an issue at the boardroom table is to bring it up at the boardroom table. There are many reasons for this. No matter how open-minded people claim to be, human beings are usually resistant to change. What's more, throwing a great idea out to a room full of people *without getting buy-in first* is the ultimate in go-it-alone tactics. While it may *seem* like a quicker option to simply share your idea with several people all at once, your idea will not go as far. I know this from (painful) experience.

It was my second senior leadership meeting with Arthur Blank, plus a suite of other senior leaders from the Canadian team. We were going over our quarterly numbers. They weren't great, but I was optimistic we could turn things around in the next quarter. I had just spent several months on the front lines of Home Depot Canada stores, talking to customers and employees and getting a solid handle on how the business was run. And I had some ideas I wanted to share that I believed would help to drive sales.

Specifically, I thought all the aisles should be numbered and labelled—similar to what you now see in grocery stores—so that customers could easily find their way around. It might seem like an obvious idea today, but in the mid-'90s, numbered aisles weren't the norm. Also, to accelerate store openings, I wanted to introduce prefabricated "Depot Dons," big, sandwich board–style signs that included detailed descriptions of how to do a particular home improvement project. I thought these ideas were brilliant and wanted to push forward with them as soon as possible. And if I'm being really honest, I was still new in the saddle and wanted to reinforce to the senior leadership team that Arthur Blank had made the right decision in hiring me, as evidenced by the amazing ideas I was about to unleash. And so, without consulting anyone beforehand, I tabled my suggestions during our meeting, blithely assuming I'd get rapid buy-in and support. Contrary to my expectations, I got my head served to me on a platter. The general consensus can be summed up in one colleague's assessment: "Annette, these are really stupid ideas."

For those of you who have not worked in old-school corporate environments, this "feedback" probably sounds incredibly harsh. But as anyone who has spent time in corporate boardrooms can attest, business discussions can be painfully blunt. Being told my ideas were "stupid" was hardly the worst criticism I got at a meeting. Besides, I'd rather know exactly where someone stands on an issue than have them pussyfoot around me in an effort to spare my feelings. I left that meeting with a badly bruised ego, but also with a truckload of new insight about the pitfalls of going it alone.

## RIDING SOLO LEADS TO MISCALCULATION

Credibility is the invisible social capital you build over time that allows people to give you the benefit of the doubt needed to support a bold idea. Because leadership so often involves choosing actions or strategies that are new, bold and unproven, credibility as a leader is critical.

Any time that you table an innovative course of action, you are leveraging your credibility, putting it on the line. Just as you never want to overleverage yourself financially, you do not want to overleverage your credibility, either—which is exactly what I did when I pitched an idea that was deeply disruptive to the "Home Depot way" of doing business. So how do you reduce the risk of pitching your innovative ideas and simultaneously boost the odds that they will actually see the light of day? By enlisting support from others and pitching as a *team*. Don't bring your best ideas up to a cold room. Figure out who will be at the meeting and approach some of the more influential people with whom you have a solid relationship. Run your idea by them, ask for feedback and win their support. Only when you have support should you—as team, not as an individual—table a bold new idea to a group.

This is a smart, team-centric approach. And it's not the approach I took at the meeting in question. Had I discussed my ideas with others before the big meeting, in an effort to get feedback and support in putting them forward, I would have learned an important lesson. The first was that one of the unspoken rules at Home Depot was that store associates should spend as much time speaking to customers as possible and that anything that interfered with these discussions was frowned upon. So my idea of posting signs to make the stores easier to navigate was shot down because the signs would remove a reason for an associate to speak to a customer. Had I known about this beforehand, I could have addressed the concern while I was pitching my idea. Without this knowledge, I miscalculated my pitch, and my credibility took a small, though temporary hit, easy to overcome through hard work and results but not a mistake I wanted to repeat.

*YOU RISK OTHERS "PILING ON"*

It is an unfortunate consequence of power dynamics that people will rarely disagree with the top dog and will instead reinforce that person's decision. In the early 2000s, corporate culture was dog-eat-dog, no matter where you worked. In some corporate environments, that atmosphere is still alive and well today. There were people at that table who wanted my job. By taking Arthur Blank by surprise with a very different approach, I opened up the door for others to follow his lead and criticize me roundly. Now, criticism happens and you can't run your career avoiding criticism; if you did you would hardly be a leader. But as much as possible, you want to choose your battles carefully. There are times I'm prepared to take criticism because I'm putting forth an idea I soundly believe in. But in this case, I would have been better off testing out my ideas with a few people individually before the meeting to gauge the temperature, rather than going it alone and getting blindsided.

*YOU DIMINISH YOUR ABILITY TO BRING YOUR GREAT IDEAS TO FRUITION*

Leadership is intangible. Sure, you may have an impressive title, but so did Louis XVI. Titles bestow a certain amount of power, but you can't lead a team if others don't wish to follow you and embrace the ideas and solutions you bring. Your ability to lead is based on your skill at influencing outcomes. And the ability to influence outcomes is deeply tied to your relationships; in other words, influence is dependent upon teamwork. In the "Depot Don" meeting, my choice to go it alone directly resulted in a lack of influence. Had I had others on my side before I presented my idea, they may well have gone to bat for me, and as a team we could have brought forth a solution to drive sales together. This is the age-old "power in numbers" approach. By going solo, I diminished my influence and my ideas couldn't pass muster. Not at the time, anyway. A few years later, every Home Depot store in Canada had numbered aisles and prefabricated "Depot Dons." But I never again brought bold new ideas to a meeting without warming up a portion of the room first.

## TEAMWORK IN ACTION

The work I do today in energy storage is highly innovative and rapidly evolving. Technological developments outpace governments' ability to develop policies to both regulate the industry and to bring clean energy technology online. Meanwhile, the world is facing an urgent need to deal with our dependence on fossil fuels. When I got into the business, years of "Depot Don" experiences had taught me that the only way to carve out a successful niche not only for NRStor, but also for the clean-technology industry, was to collaborate. Put another way, my ability to successfully lead this company was based on my ability to unite a diverse team of people who normally would not collaborate and work toward the common goal of growing the energy storage industry.

When I took a look around at the energy storage landscape, I saw a group of small, high-potential companies trying—and failing—to influence government separately. This never works. If you want to get things *done*, especially anything that is new, radical or innovative, strength in numbers is critical. We had to build a team that went beyond

NRStor employees, but also included our competitors, stake-holders and supply chain, so that when we went in to discuss energy storage regulation or options with governments, we presented a unified front and therefore had clout. So I pushed hard to work with other energy storage companies, research groups, energy consultants and developers to create Energy Storage Ontario. Our mission is to advance the energy storage industry as a whole, so that we can collectively benefit. We have been able to influence the Ontario government to include fifty megawatts of energy storage in its long-range energy plan for the province.

Ironically, when you find ways to collaborate with people and groups outside your normal sphere of influence in support of a collective goal that's bigger and loftier than your own individual gain, you truly distinguish yourself as a leader because you are able to achieve larger, more difficult tasks.

As you take on more leadership at work, or in your life, family or community, I invite you to shift from thinking about how you can move quickly to how you can enlist other people to work together so you can all move farther. Are you trying to move a new initiative forward? Have an idea for an exciting new project? Think of a few people with whom you can share your idea, who can help you shape it, and give your plan the support it needs to succeed. Look at the "collaborative partnerships" you have at work and in your sphere of influence and ask yourself whether you are thinking innovatively when it comes to partnerships. A basketball team made up of only guards would not be successful—you need forwards and a centre, people who bring diverse skills and play the game differently. Do you have people from diverse backgrounds and interests among your partners and collaborators? Taking the time to cast a broader net and develop partnerships and collaborations outside your sphere of influence boosts your credibility and effectiveness as a leader. It may take longer, but you travel a heck of a lot farther that way.

## THE HEART OF TEAMWORK: ENGAGING WITH PEOPLE

My brother Andy, who is smart, kind and a brilliant mechanic, struggled in school. I'm a huge believer in education and I know that for people who for whatever reason are outside "the norm," school can be a challenging—and sometimes traumatic—experience. My siblings and I all started out in a two-room schoolhouse a mile or so from the house. At one point, Dorothy, Turk, Andy and I were all in that school together. On one day in particular, Andy was having trouble. He couldn't have been much older than five or six. Something happened—perhaps he couldn't sit still, or maybe he just couldn't answer a particular question. The next thing we knew, the teacher had paraded him to the corner of the schoolhouse and plunked a dunce cap on his head. She made him stand there while the rest of us completed our school-work. I will never, ever forget the image of my little brother standing in the corner with tears streaming down his face. When the school bell rang, we formed a protective circle around Andy, took him home and told our parents what happened. They were livid. My father immediately complained to the superintendent, and soon after the teacher was replaced. What makes me so upset is that had the teacher taken time to know what Andy was *good* at, he would have felt heard and valued and chances are high that his experience in school would have been much more pleasant. Well, as pleasant as it could be for someone who hates to sit and likes to work with his hands. The bottom line: you can't teach someone if you don't know them. And you definitely can't lead people if you're not interested in getting to know them.

I am deeply curious about people. Some of this comes naturally, but I have consciously honed this quality over time because I learned that the most important aspect of leadership is creating an environment where everyone performs even better than they would on their own. Creating this environment necessarily involves working with people as individuals, to bring out their best for the team. While you may enjoy this aspect of leadership, in the run of a busy day or week, it's all too easy to look at people as "problems" that need to be solved. Years of leading teams have taught me that everyone has a story, and that performance issues or team problems usually have their root in those stories. A big part—the hardest part—of leading people is to develop the curiosity and people skills you need to understand people's stories so that you can help them be better. And when it comes to making tough personnel decisions, if you've taken the time to truly know the people on your team, you will make team decisions based upon an in-depth understanding of your team members.

During my Home Depot years, I had a senior manager that I was under constant pressure to fire. He was ambitious, hard-driving and disliked by his peers. He wanted to be the best and frequently looked for opportunities to one-up his colleagues. This behaviour was beginning to create a poisonous team atmosphere, and I knew I had to nip it in the bud. Despite his lack of popularity, I actually liked the guy. I admired his drive and energy, and what others saw as showmanship and competitiveness, I saw as possible signs of overcompensation. I invited him into my office one day and started asking questions about his work, the team environment, what challenged him and what he enjoyed doing. Over the course of our two-hour-long conversation, I learned that his father had died when he was a small child, leaving his family in tough economic circumstances. His life fell apart for much of his childhood and adolescence, and his behaviour seemed to be partly driven by a desire never to return to such difficult circumstances. In this context, his choices were more understandable, even though they were causing him and the people around him a lot of grief. I got him to agree to work with a coach, who helped him clarify his thinking and work through some of the inner obstacles that had been driving his behaviour. The impact was enormous. He kept his drive and determination, but he overcame the fears that had been driving him to compete—rather than collaborate—with his colleagues. I'm not suggesting that leaders need to become psychotherapists. I am suggesting that anyone who wishes to have the privilege of leading people has to cultivate the desire and curiosity to know people, not just the positive, happy parts, but the whole person.

The key takeaway: don't play the age-old game of compartmentalizing home and work. Use your informal meeting time with people—in the elevator, at the water cooler—to get to know who they are as individuals. Develop an understanding and appreciation of the whole person. By asking questions and demonstrating a genuine interest in your team members, you not only build trust and loyalty, you also develop the credibility and knowledge you need to support them to reach their full potential.

## THE THIRTY-PERCENT RULE

Here is an unscientific rule of thumb that I would nevertheless stake my reputation on: A person's potential is usually thirty percent higher than he or she thinks it is. Part of building a top-performing team and creating an environment in which people can do their best work is simply to share your vision of what is actually possible for them and then hold them to it.

Part of the role of leader is to create an environment where individuals working as a team outperform their efforts working alone. By raising the stakes—setting bold targets that your team can make by bringing their very best to the table—you elevate performance, create memorable wins and give people the gift of seeing what they are truly made of. Take a look at the projects you are currently engaged in. Is there an opportunity to raise the stakes by setting targets that are bolder and more ambitious than you initially thought possible? If you do set a stretch goal for yourself or your team, how will you build in the extra support needed to reach those goals? Could you set a personal target to check in with each team member on a weekly or biweekly basis? Setting bold targets and providing the necessary follow-up support can not only bring a team together, but also enhance the performance of each individual player.

## LEADING PEOPLE YOU DISLIKE

While it is rare for me to dislike people, it happens. As a leader, it's critical to be able to work with people you either dislike or don't connect with, because if you can't do that, you can't expect anyone on your team to. When interpersonal problems occur in business, it sometimes comes down to the mistaken belief that you should like everyone with whom you work. The reality is that you certainly don't have to like everyone with whom you work, but you do have to find a way to work with them.

Here is my two-step process for working effectively with people I don't immediately click with. First, I get very clear on the big goal I am working toward; in other words, I try to keep front and centre the reason why I must work with this person. Second, I develop relationships with people who *can* work with that particular person and as much as possible I work through them.

At one early point in my career, I was given express instructions from my bosses to work with someone who specialized in real estate. We got off to a rocky start and our relationship only went downhill. I'd select a site, and he'd tell me—and whoever else would listen—that it was terrible. Then he'd present me with a site, about which I felt just as unenthusiastic. I had no authority over him, nor he over me, but our mutual boss had made it clear that we needed to collaborate. After a few meetings that were less productive than I would have liked, largely due to our personality conflict, I discovered a solution. There was a man on his team—let's call him Richard—whom I liked and respected. From then on, I never had anyone from my team reach out directly to the man in question. Rather, we communicated only with Richard, who involved his boss as necessary. This minimized the personality conflict between me and Richard's boss and allowed us as a team to be more effective and make better, faster decisions. Surprisingly, by developing this "work-around" with Richard, we strengthened our relationship with the real estate arm of the business even though the head of that division and I rarely saw eye to eye. In this way, I was able to demonstrate to the firm's senior leadership that I could work effectively with anyone by setting personal differences aside and finding a way to achieve results.

Unless you're a saint, there are probably a few co-workers with whom you simply don't click. How might you involve other people in your team in order to minimize your exposure to the person in question, *while* you build strong connections and get better results? Finding ways to enlist team members to help you deal with people you find difficult is not only a team-building strategy; it also helps you create even better results, because you are tapping into a more diverse skill set. Sure, it'd be fun to lead a team of people who were all exactly like you, but chances are, with so much homogeneity, you wouldn't get the brilliant results that are possible when a diverse group of personalities, approaches and skills get together in support of a collective goal.

## GET OUT OF THE BOX—LITERALLY

You may have seen articles and advertisements for standing desks and treadmill desks, or maybe you've considered investing in a medicine ball you can use instead of a regular office chair. There seem to be hundreds of solutions designed to help people get more activity without having to actually go anywhere.

Being sedentary and confining yourself to your desk is not only bad for your health, it's also bad for your ability to build great teams. The simple act of walking is a terrific team-building tactic. At both Michaels and Home Depot, I "walked the store" with managers and associates as often as I could. Rather than just visiting a store and heading straight for the meeting room, I'd take a couple of employees and walk part of their store with them, usually peppering them with questions. I tried to do store walks with employees from different departments to ensure I was getting as complete a picture as possible of what the business looked like on the front lines. At the end of these walks, I'd ask each employee the three things they learned from our time together. I also encouraged employees within the stores to walk with each other, as a way to increase the flow of information and ideas.

Throughout the year, I'd invite employees from different departments, and of all different levels of seniority to come together for "blue sky" sessions, where we as a group discussed issues related to the business and came up with ideas for addressing them. The more opportunities I had to speak to employees, and the more I was able to help them connect with one another, the better the business results usually were. There's so much in business we can measure. But there's something immeasurable that happens when you bring people together in support of a common goal. The more you focus the bulk of your leadership efforts on building an atmosphere where everyone can unleash their full potential, the more you will see the magic of collaboration at work.

Success in leadership is about conditioning yourself to think "team" first. Give credit where it's due. Ask for insight.

Enlist support. Nurture an atmosphere where people communicate with and help one another. Ask questions and get to *know* the people you are leading. Take a few moments and write down three powerful, consistent actions you could take to enhance your team dynamics and commit to taking these actions daily. The results will astound you.

## KEY CONCEPTS

1 Retraining yourself to think, work and achieve as a team is one of the most profound, effective and career-making shifts you will make as a leader. This goes beyond simply delegating. It's about consciously looking for ways to enhance the team dynamic, and to support everyone on the team to unleash their full potential.

2 My most painful business mistakes have come about because I—like so many emerging leaders— was impatient and believed I saw a chance to move faster on my own.

3 Don't bring up your best ideas to a cold room. Figure out who will be at the meeting and approach some of the more influential people with whom you have a solid relationship. Run your idea by them, ask for feedback, and win their support. Only when you have support should you—as a team, not as an individual—table a bold new idea to a group.

# CHAPTER 11

# TAKING RISKS PAYS OFF

Your career as a leader will be marked by a series of forks in the road. And as in the Robert Frost poem, you'll usually be choosing between the predictable path and the unpredictable one. One provides certainty and security, the other involves uncertainty and risk. So which one do you take?

To paraphrase Frost, taking the (riskier) less-travelled road can make all the difference. That's because there's a positive correlation between the amount of risk a leader is willing to take, and the rewards she is able to receive. It follows that learning how to take smart risks is critical to your development as a leader.

In 2004, Home Depot was operating under the guidance of CEO Bob Nardelli, a charismatic, hard-driving man who had spent years at General Electric. Nardelli saw a business opportunity in China. At the time, China was very much considered by North American firms as the Wild West of business development: promising on account of its large and upwardly mobile populace; risky on account of big cultural differences and the instability of doing business in an emerging market. For Home Depot, the China opportunity was perceived to be especially exciting. Rising incomes and rural out-migration was creating demand for renovation and construction. Nardelli and the rest of the Home Depot leadership weighed the odds and decided that a move to China was the right one for the company, and began setting up operations. Home Depot put a team on the ground in Shanghai and they presented a strategy on how to enter China. Unfortunately, they struggled to put forward a strategy the company supported.

Early in 2006, Nardelli was replaced by Frank Blake, a quiet, steady man, and a brilliant CEO, whose strategy from the outset was to refocus Home Depot's strategy from Nardelli's emphasis on cost-cutting and growth in the wholesale business to its original focus on the centrality of customers and employees. Blake did not have the same affinity Nardelli had had for the China market, although while he was still working under Nardelli, he was charged with doing a deal that eventually led to the purchase of The Home Way, a company that built home improvement stores in China that looked and felt like Home Depot stores. (I had my suspicions that The Home Way had been built by its founders with the express purpose of being sold to Home Depot; employees wore orange aprons, the stores were orange, and a decade earlier the company had sent employees to Home Depot stores in California for training.) Frank wanted an existing Home Depot leader to run the China operations. He approached me even before he was CEO and asked if I would do it. I started working on the China entry in 2006.

Given China's emerging role in the world economy and the growth potential of Home Depot's business in the Asian market, the job was the opportunity of a lifetime. And it was risky as hell. I was ten years into my role as president of Home Depot Canada, with a solid track record behind me. China offered me a chance to lead a team that could achieve extraordinary growth for the company. But given the unpredictability of the market and the fact that many North American and European firms were struggling to get a foothold in that country, the assignment also had the potential to damage my credibility.

I was at a fork in the road. The first option was to continue running Home Depot Canada, a path that was relatively certain and secure. By this time we had expanded significantly and my work as CEO was focused on seeing our existing strategy through to completion. I had overcome many of the biggest challenges of the job—winning the respect of my peers, leading the Canadian expansion into new markets, building a solid executive team. This option was clear, achievable and known.

The second option was to augment my duties significantly by accepting the new, much riskier role of Home Depot China, where I would be leading a group of employees and serving customers who spoke an entirely different language, who lived on the other side of the world, and whose business practices I knew little about. This path offered a future characterized by risk and uncertainty.

Now you may not have been tapped to lead the expansion of an international office (yet), but I'm sure there have been times in your career when you have arrived at a similar fork in the road, where you must choose between the secure path you know and the riskier path with the unknown outcome. I'm also sure you are reading this book because you aspire to lead people to achieve tangible results. You want to make an impact. And finally, I suspect that you want to be rewarded, through recognition and compensation. For all these reasons, I invite you to consider taking the riskier path. All the career-making moves I've made have involved a lot of risk. Meanwhile, the times I have felt stymied or stagnant in my career have occurred during periods where I have been working within a relatively risk-free environment, doing work I already knew how to do. I have seen high-potential people spend their entire career in that space, out of an unwillingness to take risk. Had I not been willing to take risks, I would not be where I am today.

I accepted Frank Blake's offer to lead Home Depot Asia. My decision and subsequent experience offer some useful insights into what to do and, perhaps even more importantly, what *not* to do, when taking on risks.

## EVALUATING RISK

In Chapter 1, "Know Your Baseline," I covered the importance of knowing your values, and using that internal compass to guide your actions. Knowing your baseline is critical when it comes to evaluating and taking risks. Here's why. When we make decisions that are coherent with our values, we experience a sense of alignment. This alignment is crucial—the last thing you want when you are entering new territory is to be in a state of internal strife. Rather, you want to focus your full energy on the task at hand, not on wondering whether you've made the right decision. In my case, growth, adventure and team are all important values. So the prospect of leading the China business offered me a chance to honour all of those core values: leading a business in an entirely new country offered a tremendous learning and growth opportunity;

communicating and experiencing a different culture would be an epic adventure; the ability to use my leadership skills to support the company's expansion efforts was a team play. From my perspective, the risk was in alignment with my baseline.

Learning to evaluate decisions based on your values— rather than on, say, your emotions or even simple logic—is the hallmark of an emerging leader. But the key to building your leadership presence is to take an even larger view; you need to evaluate risk and make decisions based upon not only *your* values, but also on the needs of the organization or team you serve. I was not the only senior executive within Home Depot who felt that running the Asian division had the potential to damage personal credibility and reputation. That's why no one else had stepped up to volunteer for the role. But from Home Depot's perspective, this was a piece of business that simply had to be run well. Someone had to do it, and ideally that person was a seasoned executive from within Home Depot who understood the company's overarching vision, and who could implement that vision in an entirely new market.

You will encounter a series of risks throughout your career, and your ability to ascend into roles of increasing impact will generally correlate to your ability to be a shrewd connoisseur of risk. Here's the rule of thumb I have applied: when I find that a particular opportunity (risk) lines up not only with my values, but also with the goals of my organization, I know this is a worthwhile risk to take.

## ARTICULATE YOUR CONCERNS

Once you've done your gut check to ensure the risk lines up with your values and is aligned with the goals of your organization, it's time to get very clear on the potential dangers embedded in the move you are considering. The thing about fear is that it so often goes unspoken, which gives it more power. While many senior executives understood the opportunities inherent in leading the Asia business, I know that many were, like me, concerned about exposing themselves to such a potentially volatile opportunity. And for some people, that's as far as their exploration went. I was able to take the conversation one step further by highlighting to my boss, Frank Blake, exactly what my concerns were. My first concern was that I would be increasing my workload by at least a third. Given that I was already working long hours during the week, this was a big step up. The second concern was that, if things went south, my reputation and credibility would be damaged. Frank and I worked out a fair compensation for the additional responsibilities I took on. And importantly, he assured me that in taking on the China assignment, I was not putting my career at risk. "Annette," he said, "if this is successful, great. If it's unsuccessful, it will not hurt your career. The experience of working in China will only enhance your career." Now that I had articulated my concerns and had my boss's support, I had almost all the information I needed to make my final call.

## DO YOUR DUE DILIGENCE

For some people, "due diligence" might conjure an image of accountants sitting around a boardroom table for six months poring over hundreds of boxes of financial data. There is a time and place for this level of detailed due diligence. For most purposes, however, a simpler approach will do. In Chapter 5, "Mediocre Strategy, Brilliant Execution," I presented the idea that leadership is often about *making your decision the right one* through executing on that decision very well. Therefore, I define due diligence as the act of ensuring I have access to the resources I will need to make a particular venture successful. Specifically, I need the answers to three questions:

1. ***Do I have the ability to put the right people in place?*** I wanted to ensure I had the leeway to shuffle people around internally so that I was surrounded by people I trusted when it came to building the business in China. Your ability to take a risk and be successful is linked to the strength of the team you have surrounding you. It follows that a prudent element of your due diligence is taking stock of the talent pool from which you can draw.

2. ***Do I have enough capital to do what needs to be done?*** Before I said yes to the China assignment, I had a serious conversation with Frank Blake about how much capital Home Depot was willing to allocate to the Chinese expansion. I had a broad sense of what needed to be accomplished, and that gave me a reasonable expectation of how much capital I'd need to make that strategy happen. When it comes to capital, you always want to ensure you have enough at the outset. The beginning of a new initiative is always the easiest time to secure capital. If you don't have the money you need to execute on your plan, and you don't have a strategy to secure the money, consider whether the risk is actually worth it.

3. *Am I protected?*

One of the simplest ways to protect yourself and hedge risks you take is to set specific timelines around the work. I ensured I had a solid contract laying out my responsibilities as the president of Home Depot Asia, and we set a specific timeline, giving myself three years in the role. I also negotiated for more compensation, given the additional workload, as well as for the ability to train some key Chinese workers in Canada to help with the entry into market.

In late 2006, I became president of Home Depot Canada and Asia. It was a whole new chapter in my professional life; I travelled to China almost monthly, spending roughly a quarter of my time in that country as we set to work "fixing" the business, while I maintained the Canadian operations with the support of an experienced leadership team.

From the outset, China proved a difficult market. My first job was to put the right leader in place at the local level. I hired a Chinese national who had been working at French multinational retailer. Together, he and I launched into our strategy of building Home Depot China. We examined our supply chain, upgraded the stores and trained our employees. We had great people—they were hard-working, extremely committed and followed their training to a T. However, understanding the tendency of our Chinese workforce to follow instructions to the letter was one of my biggest cultural learnings. One day, as I did a store walk with several employees, I mentioned that the store looked cluttered and said that too many pallets were being used as displays. The next time I returned to the store, they had all been removed; there wasn't a single pallet in sight. This wasn't ideal, as it meant that in-store floor displays were now non-existent.

I learned to be extremely mindful of my words when I spoke to employees. I grew up in a culture where there is an inherent understanding of the "grey area." In China, my experience was that there was little grey area; communication was much more black and white. If I asked for something to be done when I walked through a store, it would often be done—completely—by the time I left.

Despite the cultural differences, working with our employees was the highlight of my experience in China. I remember that each morning store staff would do group calisthenics in the parking lot outside the store. They had formalized processes for boosting morale such as group meetings and cheers; as a team-centric person, I enjoyed this level of enthusiasm. Unfortunately, our tremendous workforce could not make up for the deep challenges we faced. We were up against international competitors with more years in the market and with state-owned home improvement stores that offered similar products at subsidized prices. We employed Home Depot's strategy of targeting home owners and do-it-yourselfers. Our "assortments," or product lines, were targeted to this type of consumer. But in China, where there was an abundant supply of low-cost labour, there was a minimal do-it-yourself market; people usually hired contractors for even the smallest home improvement jobs. We didn't stock contractor-specific assortments, which meant our inventory was not turning over anywhere near fast enough to make a profit. What's more, unlike in North America, where assortments were more or less the same across stores, with specific regional differences, in China the assortments needed to vary on a city-by-city basis. Unfortunately, we offered the same assortments in practically every store. To complicate matters even more, bookkeeping and inventory control were done manually, and there were no credit or electronic payments—cash and cheque only—which meant we had trouble pinpointing our exact position on any given day, information that is critical to a retailer attempting to diagnose specific problems and fix them.

Shortly after I arrived, I discovered that the previous owners had run the business very differently from the Home Depot way. Vendors would sell product to us at one price, then sell the same product much more cheaply elsewhere. Our stores became a grand showroom; a place to visit and view, but not to buy. Furthermore. Home Depot did not own the real estate upon which our stores stood, a situation that led to no end of strife. On one occasion, after we refused our Beijing landlord's request to make changes to a particular store, our power was cut off. In 2008 the government planted trees throughout our store parking lot in an attempt to make it attractive for the Olympics. I understood the reasoning, but it created a logistical challenge for delivery trucks and customers. Together, these challenges were hurting our ability to profitably run the existing business, much less expand. Soon after arriving, we closed down two of the stores in an effort to boost profitability.

Close to two years into the assignment, I saw that despite our very best efforts our strategy wasn't working, and we decided to close another three stores. It was a complicated time for me personally. On the one hand, the extreme challenges were a source of stimulation; I loved being immersed in a new culture, and working with my team in such a focused, all-hands-on-deck way. On the other hand, I was deeply concerned about Home Depot's future in that country, and felt badly for the employees who had lost their jobs. As much as I believe that leaders can demonstrate power through vulnerability, I did not want my team to see the concern I felt, nor did I hide the gravity of our situation from them. I focused on projecting a calm, confident energy even as I laid out what was at stake, and asked for ideas and input on how to overcome the hurdles. By that time, I had completed my timeline and done my best to stabilize the China expansion. From an operational perspective, we saw big improvement, but the merchandising, distribution and sales strategy did not meet our targets. Bill Lennie, who ultimately succeeded me at Home Depot Canada, worked with me for a year, helping to address these challenges.

Frank Blake and I agreed that it was time to step down from Home Depot Asia in 2009. I needed to focus on Home Depot Canada as we embarked on a massive technological upgrade that needed my full attention—as well as that of my team. To Home Depot's credit, it stayed in China another four years. Bill Lennie replaced me in Asia, followed by the company's CFO Carol Tome, who closed Home Depot Asia in 2012.

## DEBRIEF—BUT DON'T SPEND TOO LONG STARING AT THE REARVIEW MIRROR

It's one thing to experience a setback, it's another to learn from it. After I left China, I took some time to reflect on what went wrong. My attempt to make Home Depot Asia a success was one of the few things I have ever taken on that fell short. It hurt. The environment was incredibly tough. I was on boards of companies that had attempted to penetrate the Chinese market, so I was well aware of the challenges and failure rate of Western companies in that part of the world. All those things had presented me with a very real conundrum, but they were a bit out of my control. Two things had been in my control, however. The first is that I questioned whether I had done enough personal due diligence before taking on the assignment. Before I took on the role, I relied on financial statements, the few trips I had taken to the market beforehand, and my colleagues' impressions. Looking back, I think it would have been a good idea to look further into the market, in order to ensure the expectations I set for myself and my team were reasonable. But perhaps the biggest personal decision I questioned was my choice not to live full-time in China during my tenure as president. To this day, I wonder whether becoming a local— at least temporarily—would have made a difference.

Maybe it's my relentless optimism, or perhaps it's a function of my pragmatism, but I simply do not view my China experience as a failure. I wish I had been able to help Home Depot make its foray into Asia a long-term success. I still think of the great employees we laid off after closing five stores. But when I do look back at the experience, I remember the wonderful team I worked with, I recall all the tremendous business lessons I learned and continue to apply today, and I have a sense of gratitude that life afforded me the privilege of leading and working in another country.

The upside of risk is reward, the downside is failure. As a leader, it has been my job to learn from my so-called failures, and ultimately to move on. I have seen many a great career derailed by the choice to lament what could have been. If you spend too long staring at the rearview mirror, you can destroy your confidence and your desire to take further risks. Taking risks is a little like learning how to ride a bike. Fall off? Then you need to get back on straight away so you don't lose your nerve. Self-doubt is normal human behaviour, but it can be lethal to your success as a leader. The trick isn't to try and *avoid* self-doubt, but to notice when self-doubt does creep into your thoughts and make a conscious decision to focus on the present.

## ADVANCED NINJA TACTICS FOR HEDGING RISK

If there is one behaviour you can consistently implement to give you the foundation you need to hedge the risks you take throughout your career, it is without question, the habit of building relationships.

In 2008, Home Depot decided to introduce an SAP (data processing) system. At the time, the company's American and Canadian operations were tangled in a complex technical web of more than eighty different legacy systems, none of which were integrated, leading to even more inefficiencies. The senior leadership team in Atlanta believed a new SAP system would reduce inventory and integration headaches and boost profitability, and they had struck a deal with Accenture to implement the system. But before the system could be safely introduced into the U.S. market, the company needed to test it out. The U.S. market was ten times the size of the Canadian market; for this reason, we figured collectively that Canada would be an ideal testing ground.

The risks to Home Depot Canada's business were considerable. We were moving all of our computerized systems off the existing grid onto a completely new one. We had a date when we would basically flip a switch, and there would be no way to test if this switch-over would be successful beforehand. If there was a glitch in the system, it was possible the business could experience a blackout, complete with cash register breakdowns, data loss and just about every other retail doomsday scenario you could imagine. For the second time in as many years, I was presented with a situation where disaster was a very real danger; my reputation was on the line yet again.

I could have pushed back on my colleagues and insisted that we test the system out on, say, a region of the U.S. market. But I knew that the new system was very much the right move for the business. Furthermore, I believed that we were efficiently run and well coordinated in Canada that we were truly the best place to test out the software, despite the inherent risks. And so in 2009, the Canadian operations of Home Depot launched into the eighteen-month plan to completely overhaul the IT underpinnings of the business.

The biggest risk you face anytime you introduce change is less the technical aspect, which in this case was the ability of all the various software components to "talk to each other." Rather, the biggest risk is getting the *people* to talk to each other, share information effectively and embrace the change.

There's a military concept that I love. It states that during peace times, armies can be run very efficiently with a small group of well-trained managers, but in the fog of war, solid leadership is required at every level. And so it was during our SAP overhaul. During those eighteen months, I invested even more time in nurturing my relationships with employees of every level within the company, to ensure the set-up and adoption of the system were successful, I *needed* champions from diverse job functions within the company. I also spent a lot of time with Mike Rowe, Canadian VP of finance, who was the operational lead on the project. We built a high level of trust, which minimized miscommunication and ensured excellent coordination between Home Depot and the companies providing the software and development. The project was a massive amount of work on the part of thousands of people—but when we flipped the switch in 2010, it worked.

## RISK AS THE RIGHT NEXT MOVE

Risk has a reputation for seeming "crazy" or "out of left field," which is perhaps why it has such a bad reputation. I have found that risk is more likely to show up as the right, but difficult, course of action. There's a lot of information out there about how to lead. In my experience, true leadership isn't about how much you *know*. Rather, it's about having the courage to act. Consider your life, work, or organization right now. Are there things you know should be done that aren't getting done? Specific initiatives that could make all the difference to your team or business? Sometimes the thing that comes in between the thing we know needs to be done and our actually doing it, is the courage to take a risk.

I have outlined some strategies to help you evaluate and hedge your risks. But developing the courage to actually take that risk is something you must do on your own. Take it from this risk junkie: I've consistently taken the risky path. And that has made all the difference.

## KEY CONCEPTS

1   There's a positive correlation between the amount of risk a leader is willing to take and the rewards she is able to receive.

2   Perform careful due diligence before adopting risk.

3   Debrief—but don't spend too long staring in the rearview mirror.

# CHAPTER 12

# GET COMFORTABLE IN YOUR SKIN: TELL YOUR STORY, OWN YOUR BRAND

Hands down, the most important asset I have is my reputation. It has taken years to build and it wasn't created by accident. Job after job, one relationship at a time, my reputation as a leader and friend has been cemented by putting my best foot forward again and again.

Many years into my career, I began hearing a new term bandied around business circles: personal brand. At first, I didn't like the word. Felt too slick. I didn't have a "brand," I was just me. Branding felt packaged and overproduced, like an airbrushed studio shot. "Reputation," on the other hand, felt authentic, me in the flesh. But as my understanding of personal brand has evolved, I've become a firm believer in its importance. Here's how I define it: your personal brand is simply your reputation in a suit—the best version of you, smartly dressed and ready for public consumption. I'm the same old Annette whether I'm in shorts and a T-shirt, laughing it up with my brothers and sister, or when I'm dressed to the nines to give a speech. One version is just a little (or a lot!) more polished. What's inside hasn't changed.

In this age of twenty-four-hour news and social media, cultivating a solid personal brand is more important than ever before, especially for emerging leaders. According to a 2012 study by the global public relations consultancy Weber Shandwick, roughly two-thirds of customers surveyed say their perception of a CEO is directly linked to their perception of the company as a whole. Further research from the company suggests that sixty-three percent of a company's market value is attributed to its reputation, and it can take three and a half years for a company's value to recover from a damaged reputation. In today's world, cultivating a strong personal brand isn't just something you do for you. It's something you do for your company *and* the two or two thousand people you represent. Your personal brand isn't self-promotion—it's a critical element in how you serve. Getting it right begins when you understand that when it comes to leadership, you're representing more than just yourself.

## BECOME THE FIGUREHEAD

Growing up, I had three sets of clothes: barn clothes, school clothes and church clothes. My barn clothes always smelled of cows, no matter how often we washed them. My school clothes were always clean, but not necessarily fancy. And my church clothes—well, they were my Sunday best. (Or more often, my sister Dorothy's hand-me-down Sunday best). Some days, especially if I was in a rush, I might head off to school without having taken a shower. But I never went to church when I looked (and smelled) anything less than my best. That's because when we went to church, my siblings and I knew that we weren't representing just ourselves, we were representing our family. Somehow, this mattered more.

We behaved better, were more patient than usual, and took extra time with our appearance. This approach to church prepared me for my role as CEO. No matter where I am, I know that I am representing NRStor, and before that Home Depot, and before that Michaels—right on down the line to the Verschuren family farm.

Remembering that you represent something larger than yourself can be tough, especially today. We live in the age of the individual. Social media, well-intentioned helicopter parenting and the self-esteem movement have invested many of us with the belief that we are incredibly significant as *individuals*. This is absolutely true—we *are* all significant just as we are, all on our own. But when we step into a leadership role, with or without a title, our identity takes on another component. We become more than simply ourselves. We become representatives of a company, an organization, a touch point to a larger group of people. Our brand, how we act and speak and the way we treat people, becomes a reflection not only of our own values, but also of the company's and, in some cases, even of the people who work there.

This may feel intimidating at first—a completely normal response. No one is born a leader. We take our time to build our skills so that we can step into that role. Not only because it's a highly skilled role, but also because it's a highly significant role. But as you intentionally build your personal brand, you'll discover something wonderful: there will come a time when you trust yourself so completely that you will be eager to become the figurehead, and represent not just yourself, not just the company, but thousands of people as well.

## ANSWERING THE TOUGH QUESTIONS FOR HOME DEPOT

The day of Home Depot Canada's grand opening for our first store, in Victoria, British Columbia, I was slated to give a speech. We had gathered a large crowd of staff, customers and dignitaries, and the team had assembled a stage where a number of us were giving speeches. When it was my turn, I got up on stage and quickly got down to the business I love best: outlining a vision and bragging about the people around me. Suddenly someone in the back of the audience stood up and started screaming. As we say in Cape Breton, she tore a strip off me, yelling about how awful Home Depot was because we were sourcing products from countries with bad forest practices. The audience had been listening before, but now the silence in the room was deafening—all you could hear was this woman's voice ricocheting off the cement floors. Out of the corner of my eye I could see the security people advancing toward her, grim-faced and presumably ready to escort her out. I had two choices: I could let the security team escort her and complete my talk or I could engage her. No one would have blamed me for choosing the first option. As a rule, audiences don't appreciate hecklers. But I have never been one to shy away from conflict and I didn't want my staff, customers or the stakeholders and dignitaries in the audience to see me do that. I wanted to demonstrate courage, strength and rationality on my own behalf and on behalf of the hundreds of people in the audience who gave the majority of their waking hours to the company. What's more, while I neither agreed with her assessment, nor appreciated the rude way in which she chose to express it, I did respect her for having an opinion. I wanted to clearly demonstrate that I tolerated dissent and welcomed the opportunity to challenge it and respond to questions.

So I took a deep breath and I signalled to the security team to let her be. When she had finished her speech, I addressed her question. I told her that I was on Home Depot's environmental council and we were working on enhancing the overall environmental footprint of the company. This work included using our purchasing power to favour products exclusively from companies that operated with recognized forest management practices, and that had third-party certification from the Forest Stewardship Council (FSC) and others.

It was a tense, highly charged moment. Responding to hecklers or informal protest is always a stressful experience because of its unpredictability. As a leader, you simply can't afford to lose your cool publicly. But by demonstrating courage under pressure, I was able to diffuse a tense situation, and use an unfortunate incident to enhance my company's reputation even further.

## IT'S NOT ABOUT ME, IT'S ABOUT WE

The paradox of personal branding is that it gets stronger the less you think about yourself. A highly unfortunate example from Tony Hayward, former head of BP, illustrates the point. On April 20, 2010, a fire started aboard the Deepwater Horizon, a semi-submersible mobile offshore drilling unit, the result of a blowout. The rig was located in the Gulf of Mexico, thirty-five miles off the Louisiana coast. Eleven people were killed in the explosion and the Deepwater Horizon ultimately sank. Over the ensuing eighty-seven days, an estimated 4.9 million barrels of oil flowed into the Gulf, making it one of the largest accidental marine oil spills in the history of the petroleum industry. In the aftermath, as BP struggled to contain the spill and seal off the wellhead, Hayward apologized on behalf of BP for the "enormous disruption" it had caused. "There's no one who wants this over more than I do," an exhausted Hayward told reporters. "I'd like my life back." Two sentences that Hayward will surely regret for the rest of his career. Eleven people had died and the Louisiana coast had suffered massive environmental devastation—and Hayward was making it all about him.

I'm not here to criticize Hayward. I have never been under such intense scrutiny nor, thankfully, will most people. But in such instances, you're relying on "muscle memory"—the behaviour you have conditioned yourself to exhibit. High-performance athletes trust years of training and preparation to help their bodies "remember" how to perform on competition day. Similarly, the way you train yourself to behave as a leader will support you during difficult times. Learning to put the interests of your customers, team or organization over your own interests will help you immeasurably. Not doing it will cost you. A few months after that fateful interview, Hayward was let go as CEO of BP.

## DON'T BE AFRAID TO ENGAGE

Some people say your reputation can be wiped out in an instant. I don't buy that—anything that is well built should be able to withstand a few storms. I have made many mistakes in my career, but they haven't cost me my reputation. The way I have handled those mistakes and the larger contribution I have made to my organizations and the people I've worked with—those are what counts.

When I first joined Home Depot, some groups of employees were trying to unionize. Winning the hearts and minds of your team members is critical and I wanted to support the company's employees as much as I could. Deep down, the senior management believed that we did represent the best interests of employees. We didn't need unions. People were angry with me for taking this stance, but I didn't back down, nor did I hold back from engaging with those who held different opinions. For six months, I travelled the country, visiting store after store, hosting town hall meetings, listening to employees and presenting our case. It was a worrisome time: only fifty-one percent of employees needed to support unionization in order for organized labour to move forward. But my tactic of getting out there and engaging worked. We were able to bring the two sides together, and develop a strong enough connection between management and employees that the majority felt—as I did—that unions weren't necessary.

## DON'T BE AFRAID TO RISK IT

Dig into the lives of the world's most revered humans, and you'll see they were all, well, *human*. Celebrated entrepreneur, visionary and leader Steve Jobs was adored by the world, and was also known for being occasionally cruel and even deceitful to the people he worked with most closely. Was it right? No. Did it permanently tarnish his reputation? No—because he stood for something greater, and because the humanity in us is capable of seeing past the mistakes to the greater contributions exceptional people make to society.

My point is this: safeguarding your reputation is not about being perfect at all times. I have seen many a leader (in title, anyway) shy away from tense or difficult situations because they were concerned about the impact on their reputation. But by not engaging, these people actually dealt their reputations a deadly blow. Personal branding is about standing for something, showing courage, taking the high road and speaking through your actions and accomplishments.

As I discussed in Chapter 1, getting crystal clear on your values is essential inner work for any leader. But your personal brand is the place where you transform those values from words on a page or thoughts in your head into decisions and actions. Compassion is an important part of my personal brand. Simply put, I treat people well and fairly. Over the years I have had to make tough decisions about people. Once I chose to let go one of my most brilliant employees because an action he had taken was completely misaligned with the company's values. I didn't shy away from making the call, but I treated him with compassion and kindness and did my best to ensure he landed on his feet. He was disappointed, but he respected how I handled the decision and he is one of my greatest supporters and friends today.

The biggest threat to my reputation (and Home Depot's reputation) occurred in 2002 during the Tent City issue. Compassion and fairness were part of my values and my brand, but I was personally divided over what the compassionate and fair decision was in that instance.

You probably haven't thought of the great country singer Dolly Parton as a leadership guru. Yet there's a quote attributed to her that underscores the point I'm making here: "Find out who you are and do it on purpose." As a leader, you will have people observing you, following you, and looking to you for guidance. This requires emerging leaders to step up and inject their daily activities with much greater levels of intention than ever before. This advice is not about developing an inflated sense of who you are. I always recommend humility. However, as a leader you are fulfilling a role. In my experience, this is a role best filled with a deep sense of purpose.

## KEY CONCEPTS

1   In today's world, cultivating a strong personal brand isn't just something you do for you. It's something you do for your company *and* the two or two thousand people you represent.

2   Learning to put the interests of your customers, team or organization over your own interests will help you immeasurably.

3   Personal branding is about standing for something, showing courage, taking the high road and speaking through your actions and accomplishments.

# CHAPTER 13

# A WORD FOR WOMEN

I had been working at DEVCO for several years in increasingly senior roles before I was promoted to the role of assistant to the president. This was not an administrative role; it was an operational one—a senior position within the organization. Shortly after DEVCO was restructured and George Currie appointed as acting president, he called a team meeting. The heads of various departments—including some people with whom I had little contact—piled into the boardroom. As usual, I was the only woman. I was about to take my seat when someone piped up, "I'll take mine black, thanks, Annette."

Whether he was trying to egg me on or honestly thought my role was to fetch the coffee, I wasn't sure, nor did I care. I took my seat, told him anyone was welcome to fix their own coffee and waited for the meeting to start.

Years later, I sat in another boardroom, this time at Home Depot's head offices in Atlanta. I was attempting to voice my opinion on a particular business strategy and no one was listening to me—it was as if someone had pressed the mute button but it only worked on me. I eventually turned to Arthur Blank and said, "How would you like sitting around with fourteen women who weren't listening to your perspective?" He intervened on my behalf and got my colleagues to listen, but I was frustrated that I had to ask in the first place.

I could tell you a hundred stories like this. Any senior woman in business could. The "networking" meetings we didn't attend because they were at strip clubs. The times— too many to count—that we were expected to take the minutes, clean up after the meeting or fetch the coffee simply because we were women. The unwanted sexual advances we had to stave off while still preserving our working relationships. The list goes on. I won't bore you with the anecdotes because, to be quite honest, it's nothing you haven't heard before. We are now in a time and place in our evolution where our society is very aware of the challenges women face getting ahead at work. But all this awareness doesn't seem to be making a huge impact.

According to research from Catalyst, an international organization that advocates for enhanced professional opportunities for women, women graduates one year out of college and working full-time earn $35,296 compared to $42,918 for men, and women hold 4.4 percent of CEO positions at S&P 500 firms. This is of concern not only for women or parents of young women just entering the workforce. This is troubling for all of us. I believe in equality and I am also an enduring pragmatist. We need more women in senior leadership positions not simply because it's the right thing to do, but also because the challenges our world is facing—massive inequality, overpopulation, environmental degradation and violence—all require unprecedented levels of creativity and innovation. Diversity breeds innovation.

Ensuring we have more women at decision-making tables isn't a "nice to have." It's an imperative.

In this context, I'm something of a unicorn. I've been CEO of large companies, I worked my way up through male-dominated industries, I sit on a number of high-powered boards. I have a seat at the decision-making tables. Because of this, I have a unique perspective on what it takes to get a seat at the table and ensure your voice is heard. It boils down to this: Be yourself, don't take anything personally and ask for what you want. Simple, right? But like all simple advice, following it can be hard to do. It doesn't have to be.

## YOU'RE A WOMAN—EMBRACE IT

I launched my career in the age of the power suit. Shoulder pads that wouldn't fit through a door. Severe style. The prevailing wisdom was that to make it in a man's world, you had to look like one. You had to be tough, hard and no-nonsense. The irony of having women acting like guys was that we were ignoring a major law of business: the law of competitive advantage. If you're a woman in senior leadership, that in itself is a competitive advantage for many reasons, but most obviously because of its rarity. Use that. I sure did. I believe I got where I am today not in spite of being a woman, but *because* of it. Sure, being female made life tougher in some cases. But my gender also gave me many distinct advantages.

Emotional intelligence (what some call EQ) is hugely important for a leader, and I'm going to go out on a limb and say that women have more of it. We just do. I've seen it time and again—we are better listeners, we're more empathic and our deeply ingrained social skills allow us to pick up not only on what's being said but, just as important, what isn't being said.

I used these highly attuned social skills throughout my career. When I want to push a point or influence an outcome that requires the buy-in of many people, I know I'll be more successful if I do it one on one to key players in a room. Yes, it's important to make your arguments and push forward and back amongst your teams and colleagues, but sometimes you need to read the audience and select those that resist and make a point to connect one on one with them. I remember in my early days at DEVCO, I had four bosses in four years. Talk about needing emotional intelligence! It was a negative business environment. The government was tired of funding this Crown corporation, so the mood was always tough. There was a lot of union–management tension. My last boss was Joe Shannon, an extremely successful entrepreneur who was asked to run the coal company. I had tried to set up a number of meetings with him but he refused, he was always too busy. Meanwhile, the pile of issues and paperwork on my desk was so high people couldn't see me when they walked into my office. Whenever he was attending a meeting I was at, I carefully observed him. He was direct and very action oriented. After one of these meetings I cornered him and said, "Mr. Shannon, you and I have a pile of work to go through. I need three hours of your time and I promise you we will get up to date. It will help you see all the issues you face and help us solve them together." He gave me my three hours. I saw that I needed to be direct with him, give him a time frame and tell him why it was needed. If I kept asking him for a meeting by notes and calls, I would probably have never sat down with him and we might not have found the mutual respect we have today.

Another, less frequently discussed advantage of being a woman in business: the interest factor. There are lots of things that can make us interesting—our experience, our uniqueness, and, in some cases, simply what we look like. I say the interest factor comprises all three, plus whatever element you bring to the table. Before I had made a name for myself, there were many instances in which men helped me or took meetings with me because they were curious. These guys met with men all day long, so I was unusual, out of the ordinary. I always welcomed this phenomenon—if people met with me or made time with me because they wanted to see a woman in action, that was fine with me. My skills would speak for themselves.

There are some people who object strongly to using the interest factor to advantage in business. They worry that using sex appeal to your advantage when relating to members of the opposite sex (if you're straight) or the same sex (if you're gay) can put you into an awkward or even unprofessional situation. While this apprehension makes perfect sense in textbooks and HR policy guidelines, it doesn't actually pan out in the real world. The reason: you show me a person who says they check one hundred percent of their sexual energy at the office door, and I'll show you a person with an honesty problem. I'll take it one step further: over the course of my thirty-nine-year-plus career, I've worked with dozens of men who made it known—some more appropriately than others—that they had sexual feelings for me. Was this "professional"? No, but it was human. And if I had complained about a lack of professionalism each and every time a man expressed interest in me, there's no way I would have made it to the corner office. I simply wouldn't have had the time. You may think my view is controversial—I believe it's pragmatic.

## UNWANTED ATTENTION

I have occasionally been the object of unwanted male attention, particularly when I was starting my career in the 1970s. In some cases the attention was well within the bounds of appropriateness—for instance, I might catch a colleague looking at me when he thought I was distracted by something else. When I worked in the coal division at DEVCO, it was considered a bad omen for a woman to go underground—absenteeism would increase on the days I was scheduled to tour the mines. Sometimes, however, the attention was hugely inappropriate.

In one instance, I was in meetings with some colleagues. We were staying at a swanky hotel and the group of us met up later for dinner. We were joined by some VIP associates who were working with us on some major initiatives. Slowly people began leaving until it was just me and one of the male associates at the table. I quickly got up to leave and he offered to walk me to my room. I told him it wasn't necessary, but he insisted, saying he'd feel "safer" if he escorted me there. I reluctantly agreed. When we got to my room, he asked me if he could come in. I said no. He became more insistent, at which point I pushed him away, went into my room, slammed the door shut and locked it.

I saw him the next day at a working group. I decided to pretend the night before hadn't happened—this was an important meeting and I'd spent weeks preparing a proposal. When I started to deliver my proposal, he quickly shut it down and asked that we move on to the next agenda item. It continued this way for the rest of the meeting.

In that moment, I was faced with a dilemma. Do I launch a formal complaint (which I had every right to do)? Do I remain in the working group and let him waste my time? Or do I move on to better pastures? I opted for the third choice. I resigned my spot on the committee and moved on to other work where I was able to make much faster progress. I didn't mention the incident to anyone.

There are many people who would disagree with my approach. They might even criticize a woman in my position for not holding a colleague publicly accountable for inappropriate conduct. They have a point. Today, I would absolutely have opted to document and perhaps formally complain. But as I've mentioned before, thirty years ago sexual harassment was tolerated to a degree we don't see today. And yet, I believe it's up to every professional woman to decide for herself how she will handle sexual attention at work. In my case, I opted to let the attention slide right off me. What my colleagues or bosses felt about me was *their* business, not my business. I treated it that way—always being my positive, enthusiastic self, and generally ignoring any sexual attention I got. When I was targeted with inappropriate behaviour, I always applied the "Not good, not bad, only better" mindset. I didn't ask myself if the person in question had behaved rightly or wrongly. I asked instead what I could do to make it better. Sometimes making things better involved removing myself from the situation, as in the story I describe above. Sometimes it involved taking decisive, unofficial action—like the time I described in an earlier chapter when I wrote a letter to a male colleague's wife detailing his inappropriateness and threatened to deliver it if he didn't rescind his lies about me. And while I have never launched a formal complaint against a co-worker, I know many women who have, and I strongly believe that in certain circumstances this course of action is the one most likely to improve the situation. I firmly believe that in focusing on how to make things better, I was able to see a much broader range of creative responses to the challenge of how to deal with inappropriateness. The key, I believe, is ensuring we pick our battles. There's no place in the workplace for sexual harassment, but your career isn't a sprint, it's a marathon. Preserving your energy by choosing which battles you'll engage in and which you'll simply ignore is critical.

## GET IN OVER YOUR HEAD

It wasn't until I worked at Den for Men that I experienced working with other women. In my other roles, women had been a rarity. That's when I began noticing what felt to me like very strange behaviour: smart, competent women who just didn't realize how brilliant they were. As you may have gathered by now, confidence has never been a problem for me. I've always felt like I was up to the challenge—even when I probably wasn't. (In which case I trusted in my ability to learn fast.) I remember working with an associate at Home Depot who simply didn't appreciate her value. She came across as timid and quiet, so others easily missed the contributions she was making to the organization. I pushed to have her promoted, and spent time with her, encouraging her to speak up and volunteer for stretch assignments. She listened to me and within a few years she had won the recognition of her peers.

What I saw in this associate was a phenomenon I have since seen in other talented women—a mistaken belief that they have to be perfect in order to be "worth promoting." A growing body of research points to the fact that women often feel they need to fulfill virtually all the criteria written on a job description in order to apply for a promotion, while men aim to hit sixty percent. Having been on the side of the table reviewing candidates for promotions, I can tell you that statistic plays out in the real world.

It didn't hold true for me, however. As I've shared previously, when I jumped feet first into NRStor and the world of energy storage, I met *less* than sixty percent of the criteria that might reasonably be expected for the founder of a company reliant on technology. I was not an energy storage expert. But I had solid leadership skills and, perhaps most importantly, I was willing to get in over my head, make mistakes and not be perfect. And of all of these things, my willingness to not be perfect was probably the most important.

Speed is important in business—especially today. If you have an idea and you sit on it, fiddling with your strategy until you get it perfect, you can be certain someone else is taking that imperfect idea and throwing it against the wall to see what sticks. I think this is a success strategy women could stand to use a little more. As I recently told a roomful of businesswomen, you put enough things out into the world, one of them is going to catch. When I feel sixty percent certain of something, I put it out into the world and start asking for feedback. I don't wait for my ideas to be perfect. Perfect gets to the dance when everyone else has already gone home. Perfect has no place in business or in life.

## SWIMMING LESSONS

This is probably not the first time you've been encouraged to "get out of your comfort zone." So why do so many ambitious women stay within their comfort zone, and not reach for the brass ring until they are completely certain they meet one hundred percent of the criteria? When I review my own life and consider the experiences of the many women I have supervised over my career, I think it comes down to this: in order for women to take a risk, we need to have some mechanism in place to make us feel safe. You want to jump into the deep end? You've got to learn how to swim.

Here are some tips on how to swim when you get in over your head.

### *STRETCH ASSIGNMENTS*

As often as possible, raise your hand for stretch assignments—projects that have you working outside your area of expertise, with people you don't normally work with, on initiatives that scare you a little bit. Taking on stretch assignments is not only a great way to make yourself more visible to senior decision-makers, it also trains you to swim in a relatively safe environment. For instance, if you've never been in charge of a budget before, far better to learn on a smaller team project than on a million-dollar P&L.

Sometimes a stretch assignment presents itself in the form of a new initiative your boss's boss is keen to launch. Other times, it's the job no one wants. I made my career volunteering for jobs other people didn't want. For example, when I took the reins as president of Home Depot Asia, it was considered a risky and undesirable post. These roles stretched my capacity, and in some cases they risked my reputation, but my willingness to take them on always helped solidify my credibility within my organizations, which came in handy when I later tried to win buy-in for my own ambitious plans.

In 2004 I was several years into my tenure at Home Depot Canada, riding high on our success, when I learned that head office was looking for one of its division presidents to lead its Expo Design Center. This was a super-high-end version of Home Depot, with about fifty-four stores. It was the company's attempt to go after the lucrative luxury home furnishings market. Our first year was very successful; we made a solid operating profit and I recruited an all-star team. But the business was hit hard by the 2006 housing crisis. Meanwhile, in its initial rollout of the Expo Design concept, Home Depot had overbuilt the stores. Cities like Chicago, which should have had maybe a single store, had five. Ultimately the decision was made to pull the plug on the stores. We closed twenty at first, and then the remaining stores by the end of 2007. I was disappointed but not defeated—I knew I had given it everything I had, and I'd learned a huge amount from trying. Expo Design Center had great leaders and they became Home Depot store managers. Many of their ideas and best practices were also incorporated into Home Depot stores. And rather than losing credibility because of my "failure," my willingness to take on the tough assignment convinced the senior leadership team that I was the woman to run Home Depot Asia, which I did from 2006 to 2009.

*ASK FOR HELP LONG BEFORE YOU NEED IT*

There's a rule about securing business loans: you always ask for the money before you need it. If you go looking for a loan when you're already cash strapped, no bank will look at you. The same is true when it comes to asking for help. The minute you take on a new assignment, start looking around you for prospective advisors who have the technical skills you need, or who have experience in the area you're now working in. Create a mental list of people, a personal advisory board you can turn to for guidance. Next, you want to play very close attention to the specific places where you get stuck or have difficulty. Remember, speed is everything in business. Train yourself to identify any places you get stuck then diagnose why. Do you need some context? Technical information? Someone to bounce your ideas off? Figure out what you need, then ask for it. Often I see women who delay asking for help because they want to "get all our ducks in a row," so they don't look incompetent. You know what? Take a risk and look a little incompetent. Believe me—your personal incompetence metre is calibrated much tighter than that of the people around you. What you may consider to be a question that lays bare your "ignorance" others will see as nothing more than a simple question.

When I founded Michaels with Brian McDowell and Jerry Payton, we decided that I would be president and hold overall responsibility for real estate, financing, HR and all other functions. This was 1993—a challenging economic time in Canada. I was often criticized for making the wrong choices on real estate by my U.S. counterparts. I trusted my instincts, but I also asked for lots of help from people who knew the

Canadian market—people like Phil Currie (an independent retail consultant) and Mitch Goldhar (whom I would work with again and again at Home Depot). So there were naysayers; there always are because those who see the cup as half empty have a great target in an inexperienced woman. Brian and Jerry were there to support me and we had the time of our lives building that business from scratch in Canada. Our success came from supporting one another, but also from asking for help when I needed it.

### DON'T TAKE CRITICISM PERSONALLY

I mean it. Nothing. I have a reputation for being positive, caring and fair. That said, you don't get to my position without having your share of critics. You name a language and I'll show you some choice words reserved for powerful, assertive women. When we take on a new initiative that is beyond our comfort zone, we naturally feel vulnerable. And because we're new in the game, we're bound to make mistakes. Those mistakes can lead to criticism. I have trained myself to not take criticism personally. A person's opinion tells you more about them than about you. Do I listen to criticism? Sometimes. But first I separate myself from the hurtful words and try to figure out what the person's judgment tells me about where they are coming from. Then, I consider how that information might be useful to me.

### BE A STUDENT

Getting in over your head means you need to be prepared to spend an inordinate amount of time learning. You have to humble yourself and be a lifelong learner. I'm not necessarily talking about going back to school and getting your MBA, or taking one certification program after another. The only formal certification I have is my bachelor's degree, but I have a PhD in practical knowledge and common sense. And I earned those "advanced degrees" by learning how to do effective on-the-job research, and spending much of my downtime reading.

When I first arrived at Home Depot, I was a thirty-nine-year-old outsider who knew nothing about home improvement. *Nada.* A large number of people who worked alongside me every day were less than amused by my appointment. To establish credibility, win trust and avoid a mutiny, I had to learn the ropes fast. I had to be careful whom I listened to. As a senior leader, you can quickly find yourself surrounded by yes-people. I needed people who would tell me the truth. So I spent a large amount of time on the floor, talking to customers and employees, and touring the production facilities of our suppliers, in an effort to understand *their* businesses and experiences, so that I could better understand Home Depot. My first six months I spent working with associates in every department, including a stint running a Rhode Island store beside an existing store manager. I had to find information out for myself, rather than sit back and expect it to be spoon-fed to me—sometimes by people who didn't necessarily have my best interests at heart. My advice is to seek counsel from others, but when you're beyond your comfort zone, do your own research.

If you looked in my bag right now, you'd see a thick plastic folder, my reading file (I still like paper). I also have a reading folder on Dropbox. I carry these folders with me everywhere, so that when I have downtime—if I'm on a plane (which I frequently am), or I'm in a cab—I make the most of my time by reading up on whatever information I need at that moment. During my retail career it was information on my suppliers. Sometimes it's the bio of a person I'm meeting with. It could be technical information on the batteries we use in our installation projects at NRStor. Making reading an ongoing habit has helped me stay afloat in uncharted waters.

Taking on stretch assignments and getting in over your head is crucial. But you also want to ensure you're not just getting any old experience, but the *right* experience.

### GET OPERATIONAL EXPERIENCE

If you want to get yourself on the CEO or board of directors track, you must get experience in operations. I explained the reasons why in depth in Chapter 6, "Put Yourself on the Line." But this piece of advice is worth repeating, particularly for women. According to data compiled by Bloomberg in 2014, virtually *all*—a whopping ninety-four percent—of CEOs of S&P 500 companies held a senior operations job immediately before taking the reins as CEO. Meanwhile, the majority of senior women in these organizations are not in operational jobs, but in senior positions related to finance, legal or human resources. I have witnessed many hugely talented senior women who have the passion and desire for the CEO job get passed over because they have no experience "on the line."

Here's the truth: if it hadn't been for Den for Men, I wouldn't have ever been CEO at Home Depot. I had great experience buying and selling assets and structuring deals, but I had no experience operating my own P&L prior to my operating role at Den for Men. Moving from a functional role in finance, legal or HR into a CEO role is more difficult.

The trend continues at the board level. When I look around at colleagues sitting across the boardroom table, I see a group of people who have come up the operations ranks. For instance, senior HR leaders are rarely appointed a seat on the board. This is a problem I'd like to see change, but until it does, ambitious women would do well to secure operational experience.

I believe success comes in all shapes and sizes. You may have absolutely no desire to be CEO or have a seat in the boardroom, and that's great. But if you *do* see yourself in these positions, you must pay careful attention to your career path and get yourself into an operational role. The career of Mary Barra, who is CEO and a member of the board of General Motors, is highly instructive. She spent thirty years at GM in increasingly senior operational roles including stints as plant manager and vice-president of manufacturing engineering.

What bothers me is that many emerging women leaders still don't realize the importance of watching their career path. While many large organizations are rolling out women's initiatives and saying they want more leadership diversity, important tactical information about how to cultivate a résumé worthy of the CEO job isn't getting through.

You may be a natural at marketing, HR or finance. You may be a legal wiz. But if you are currently sitting in one of these positions and desire to be CEO, you need to find a way to get into operations. In the short term, it could mean a demotion. I recently heard a story about a one-time national HR manager for a well-known Canadian food company who requested a regional line job as a way to get into operations. It was a step down but her company allowed her to keep her existing salary. Two years into it, she has gained highly valuable operational experience, and is being courted by other companies for senior operational roles. In other words, she's on the CEO track. I have mentored many women who have made similar moves, transitioning from advertising into a buying group, for instance, or moving from the Canadian head office to the U.S. head office, all in the name of getting broader experience. If you choose to take an operational assignment like that young woman did, make sure to negotiate a contract that will protect your position when you're ready to return to it.

### DON'T NEGOTIATE WITH YOURSELF

For most of my life, I have struggled with serious health complications related to my kidneys. This meant I wasn't able to have children. Because I don't have children, I have sometimes grappled with a silent gender bias: that I have been able to achieve what I have achieved *because* I didn't have children. I have no way to prove whether this is true or untrue. I tend to believe I am who I am. I expressed a deep interest in being "president" from the time I was a very little girl. I'm not sure a gaggle of kids—even kids as wild as I was—could have held me back from those dreams, though certainly motherhood might have shifted my priorities. I do have women colleagues, other high-achieving CEOs, who have healthy, well-adjusted children.

In fact, for a long time, I considered Steven, our youngest brother, to be the son I never had. He was born nine years after the rest of us and I was usually in charge of babysitting him. I was a mature looking child; there were even times when people asked me if he was my son.

Honestly, I don't care that people say it was my not having children that allowed me to be where I am today. What does bother me, however, is the way that organizations, especially large organizations, can make combining motherhood and a high-powered career so difficult. Women are still considered the primary parent. In many industries, it is still a rarity for men to take parental leave. While things are undoubtedly changing, women's careers are usually the ones temporarily sidelined when kids come into the picture.

A year ago a recruiter suggested I invite a whip-smart, highly accomplished lawyer, Jennifer Manning, to be the general counsel of NRStor. Jennifer is ambitious and determined. She told me she wanted to contribute her skills and experience to my company, and she was deeply committed to being present for her three children. She worried about working full-time at a start-up like NRStor. Start-ups are notorious for long working hours. I told her that I liked her and would love to have her join us. After consulting with her closest advisors—including her father, who encouraged her not to close off opportunities without first negotiating—Jennifer asked if we could work out a solution that served everyone. There are so many elements in Jennifer's approach that I admire. I love that she was proactive, coming to me to discuss her options. I appreciated that she shared her long-term vision for how she'd contribute to the team—it wasn't about her, it was about *us*. I loved that she invited me into a problem-solving conversation about how she could contribute in a way that suited us both. But what I love most of all is that she didn't negotiate with herself; instead she negotiated with *me*. She was clear about her professional ambitions and her personal boundaries, and she came to me and asked to find a way to make them both possible.

Together, we devised a solution, which I happen to think is brilliant. She works a very doable workday from 8 A.M. to 5 P.M. We understand that she may need to leave the office during the day for children's appointments, and so on. She can work from home if she needs to. Our only concern is that the work gets done—how she does it is up to her.

Another young woman recently asked me how I might have handled my career aspirations with the demands of raising a family. She knew I'm a family-oriented person, and that "being there" for children is vitally important. I told her that I would have approached my employers the way that Jennifer did. I'd lay out my desires and my commitment, and negotiate a way to achieve them both. Rather than negotiating a year-long contract—which simply doesn't provide enough runway to handle maternity leaves and the needs of small children—I'd negotiate a longer contract, one that included flexible working arrangements in a functional role, and build toward higher levels of operations experience.

Call me selfish, but one of the main reasons I want to see more women in top jobs isn't simply because I want to see more women reach their full potential. It's because I think women are a critical part of the change our world needs. I'm trying to build a new model of advancement that puts people and the environment *on par* with the pursuit of profit. We need many more empowered women at the table to help us make good on that vision.

## KEY CONCEPTS

1   We need more women in senior leadership posi-
    tions not simply because it's the right thing to do,
    but also because the challenges our world is
    facing—massive inequality, overpopulation, envi-
    ronmental degradation and violence—all require
    unprecedented levels of creativity and innovation.

2   Cultivate your emotional intelligence—a natural
    advantage for women.

3   Take on stretch assignments that push you outside
    your comfort zone.

# CHAPTER 14

# SUCCESS = GETTING AND STAYING ORGANIZED

If you want to bring the best of who you are to everything you do, you have to be organized. In fact, your ability to be successful as a leader is directly tied to your ability to stay organized. It's not sexy but it's true. I learned this important lesson the hard way.

For my parents, my first job out of university, economic development officer at DEVCO, was basically two steps down from being prime minister. Remember, they'd left Holland practically penniless. In graduating university with a business degree and getting a good-paying job with a Crown corporation, I was fulfilling the immigrant parents' dream of truly "making it" in their adopted land. It was a great job and I fought hard to beat out my competition. When I learned I was hired, my family and I had a little celebration on the farm. And together we decided that, since the offices were a twelve-mile drive from the farm, I'd continue to live in my parents' house. My mother was especially adamant—I could save money and, since I'd be so busy with work and therefore "wouldn't have time to cook and clean," at least she'd know I was being well cared for.

I lived at home for ten years. It was the best of times. It was the worst of times. A typical day unfolded like this: I woke up with just enough time to shower, dress and scamper to the kitchen for a hot breakfast my mother had prepared. I left the house and drove to work, where I stayed until late at night. Then I arrived home to a plate of delicious dinner my mother had kept warm for me. I didn't have a household care in the world—my laundry was done, my meals were prepared, my room was kept pristine. All I had to do was show up.

But nothing comes without a cost. And in my case, the price I paid was in the form of disorganization. Organization is a muscle: you don't turn it on and off; you have to use it, or risk losing it. Years of juggling academics and part-time work on the farm had given me good organizational skills. After a few years of being coddled by my mother, that "muscle" withered. I started to approach my days with a last-minute mentality. I occasionally forgot important dates with friends and family. I began having trouble managing more than a few projects at once. And together, all that disorganization started to make me feel uncomfortable. I realized that as much as I loved my mother's help and support, I needed to reclaim some independence and take charge of organizing my life once again.

The more organized I got, the more effective I became at work and at home. I began to observe a clear link between my ability to plan and my ability to get promoted. I learned an important lesson: leadership is an ongoing act of focus, organization and self-development. If there's one skill a high-functioning leader must master, it's the ability to stay organized. For one brief period in my twenties, my organizational skills faltered. And I'd say that period also equated to perhaps the slowest career growth I've ever experienced. In that respect I was lucky. Had I succumbed to disorganization later in my career, the consequences would have been far worse.

## GET SUPPORT

If I were to ever write a book on relationships, it would probably be about the relationship between a leader and her principal "assistant." There's a lot of information out there about the relationships between a leader and his team, between a rising star and her mentor, between the smart but unrecognized newbie and his sponsor. All these relationships are important. But one of the most important relationships you'll ever form as an emerging leader is the one with your right-hand person. Some people call this job "assistant." I call it "enabler." I have worked with my enabler Allison Blunt for more than twenty years. I honestly believe there's nothing the two of us couldn't take on together. We are in daily contact, and she is one of my closest friends. And all that trust got its start in my Home Depot days when I might as well have had a target on my back.

I was young, I was inexperienced in the home improvement world, and I'd taken the CEO position out from under a number of qualified internal candidates. To say that some people were unimpressed with my appointment—and possibly even eager for my demise—would not be an understatement. This rancour didn't surprise me, and to an extent I understood it. There are always internal candidates for any top job. In this case, there were at least two internal candidates at Home

Depot Canada who believed they had what it took to lead the organization, and were naturally disappointed they hadn't been selected. I get that. I also understood that I had to have all my ducks in a row if I wanted to prove to my colleagues and my boss the truth I already knew: that I was the right pick for the job. I simply couldn't afford any sloppiness or disorganization. To get a true sense of what it's like to walk into the top job at a multimillion-dollar national chain, all you have to do is imagine yourself strolling into a hurricane. It's scary and exhilarating, and there can be danger lurking.

Allison had been hired at Home Depot before I arrived. She'd just returned to Canada from the United Kingdom, where she'd worked in the banking world. Her husband worked in banking too and he travelled constantly, so she needed a job with reasonable hours, to be available to her two children, who were still in school. When a job as a customer service assistant in Home Depot's head office was offered, she took it.

To say she was shocked at what she saw was an understatement. Several of the office workers were running part-time businesses from their desks. An assistant took daily naps on a couch in the main meeting room. This was not the way things were done at the bank. But she was new, so she worked hard and silently observed the chaos. Shortly after I was hired as president and unbeknownst to me, Allison was given her notice. A former assistant was due back from maternity leave. And even though Allison's contract was for a full-time position, she was told she'd no longer be needed. Figuring she was on her way out, she decided to inform me about the goings-on at the office. She asked for a private conversation, which of course I granted. I appreciated her honesty and figured that I needed someone like her around me. I hired her on the spot to be my new assistant. We have worked off and on together ever since.

What makes our relationship work so well is that it is rooted in deep respect. Allison's business card says, "Associate, NRStor." If you ask her what she *really* does, she'll tell you she's an enabler of Canada's growth. I think she is spot on. I have been blessed with other fabulous assistants, Erblin Rexha and Cathy Morra. The best "wingmen" are deeply intelligent and intuitive people who can see the big picture of what you're trying to accomplish, anticipate the right next step and effectively clear away the obstacles so that you are working in your "brilliant zone." Allison sees that my vision is to use business as a mechanism for improving Canada's stature in the world. Helping me execute on that vision is a tall order and requires a specialized skill set. Understanding the true value of an excellent "assistant," how critical he or she is to your success, is an important step in getting and staying organized.

## DEALING WITH ALLIGATORS

I would love to tell you that life running a big company is rosy. But I'd be lying. If you aspire to have the corner office, at some point you're going to encounter alligators. Staying organized is one of the most effective tools for dealing with them. Because the office politics were so treacherous in my early years at Home Depot, with different people jockeying for position, I had to make building relationships a priority. I also had to keep a firm handle on who I asked to do what, as well as on the complexities of the senior organizational chart in a large, nationwide company. One of the first things Allison and I did was to create a master contact list within my personal database. Everyone on my team, and every single person I met with, were entered into this contact list. I included important personal information, such as the names of their spouse and children, and we also kept track of when I met them, what we talked about and any actions that needed to come next. On several occasions, keeping meticulous track of my many relationships helped me be prepared for important meetings. I knew exactly whom I was meeting with and I never forgot to follow up on anything I promised. It may seem simple, but this level of organization is challenging to achieve. Allison helped me create a system to do it consistently. We still use it today.

It's not enough to cultivate a strong network. You have to keep it organized. Rather than using your online address book as a storage facility for names and email addresses, use it to keep track of vital information about the people you work with. Refer to the contact page before you meet with people and pay special attention to any steps you promised you'd take. As CEO, you may meet with several dozen people each week, and many of those meetings will result in "action steps." By keeping track of your promises, you enhance your reputation as a person of your word.

If you work with an enabler, understand that his or her ability to help you is directly tied to their understanding of what you're trying to achieve. Share your vision, outline your goals. Ask for support. After I left Home Depot, I went on an extended holiday. A few months into it, I started thinking about what I might do next. I decided I wanted to use my CEO and operational skills at the board level, and I shared this aspiration with Allison. While I was away, she kept careful notes on which companies were looking for directors, especially in the sectors I told her I was interested in. When I came back from my world travels, Allison had a folder that identified a list of companies and contacts I could approach. The result: I was able to get back to work and hit the ground running after a long hiatus. Without sharing my dreams and goals with her, it would have taken me much longer to identify and secure my board seats.

## MY LIFE IS MY CALENDAR

I have worked an average of sixty hours a week for the last forty years. That's a lot of time. I travel almost every week, often multiple times per week. I receive multiple invitations to keynote or to mentor a new emerging leader each week. I'm grateful for these invitations and I offer my time as much as I can. But, as you can see, there are not enough hours in the day to say yes to everything. I have to prioritize and make sure that I set aside enough time to take care of the things that are most important to me. For this reason, I live by my calendar. Learning to "work your calendar" is a vital foundation of CEO-worthy personal organization. After two decades of leading companies, I've come up with some failsafe principles. Here's an inside look at how I use my calendar to keep me organized and ensure the things that matter most get my attention.

### FIRST THINGS FIRST

When it comes to setting up your calendar, I always advise people to begin with their values. What's most important to you? For me, my family and friends are hands down the most important. That's why I put them into the calendar first. I have a large, extended family and many friends. Allison and I put each of their birthdays into the calendar. I don't have as much time as I'd like to *see* my friends and families on their birthdays, but I do my best to nurture my relationships with them in any way I can. I set my calendar up so that the day before the birthday of someone I love, I get a reminder. I might decide to send flowers, or simply call a day ahead if I know I'm booked up the following day. For a busy person, these touch points are an important way to stay connected. You can't expect your friends to be around for you if you don't make an effort to engage, no matter how "important" you are. Next, I block out chunks of time for holidays. Every other year I take my family on a week-long holiday somewhere fun. Stan and I travel to an exotic place once or twice a year. Other than that, I spend my holidays at our log house on the Bras d'Or Lake in Cape Breton. It's our piece of heaven. Blocking off the dates at the beginning of the year ensures those holidays actually happen. Family and rest are non-negotiables. Once they're booked in, I move on to the more difficult task of allocating the rest of my time. This is where I rely on my list of objectives. And while you may know that it's important to have objectives, you might not be linking your calendar with your objectives quite the way I do.

### SET OBJECTIVES AND GET THEM IN YOUR CALENDAR

I don't multitask. People who tell you they can focus on more than one thing at once and actually be effective are, in my opinion, lying either to you or to themselves. I focus on one thing at a time. When I'm in a meeting, I do not check my smartphone. When I'm talking to someone, I give that person one hundred percent of my focus. One of the things that allows me the freedom to focus is that I have already identified my top business and personal priorities and have "calendared" them. For many years, I've kept a rolling list of five personal and five business objectives. Currently, my personal objectives are to lose five pounds, to improve my French, to renovate the basement in the log house, to reacquaint myself with a friend, and to plan a holiday. Each of these objectives aligns with specific items in my calendar. For instance, I have my workouts with my trainer booked into my calendar weeks in advance. To improve my French, I have booked a week-long holiday in Quebec with my family. I don't leave any of these goals to chance—I choose an activity that moves me toward this goal, and I book time for it. When I've achieved my goal, I cross it off the list and add another goal, so that I always have a list of five personal goals.

My current business objectives are to beat our business plan, make a decision on a new senior executive within the next six months, work on a residential and remote community energy storage strategy, and also work on an energy storage strategy for western Canada and the Maritimes. Each of these goals has specific, calendared actions associated with it. For instance, I have time earmarked in my calendar to read up on a long list of candidates I've identified for the senior executive position.

The takeaway: The higher you advance as a leader, the more important it is to hit objectives consistently and the more limited your time becomes. You can no longer afford to set a goal and *hope* you reach it. Nor can you operate in the general direction of where you want to go without setting specific goals. Set personal and professional goals, identify important actions for each and book them into your calendar. If it's not in the calendar, it simply isn't real.

Allison and I meet every Monday morning at 8 A.M. and we review the week's objectives, then take a look at my calendar three months out. If we have a critical meeting, my team and I will hold a team meeting two days' prior to ensure we are prepared. It's not enough to have everything written down—you need a routine for reviewing your calendar.

By now, staying organized and focused on my priorities is second nature. I know my calendar like the back of my hand. This level of organization allows me to stay on top of my commitments, never overbook myself, and spend quality time on the things I value most. Organization and focus will allow you, too, to bring the best of yourself to your business and your life.

## KEY CONCEPTS

1   Your ability to be successful as a business leader is directly tied to your ability to stay organized.

2   One of the most important relationships you'll ever form as an emerging leader is with your right-hand person. Some people call this job "assistant." I call it "enabler."

3   Review your calendar regularly. Plan your personal life first then prioritize business.

# CHAPTER 15

# LEAD RESPONSIBLY

Most of us use only a portion of our potential. There are lots of reasons for this, including a lack of training, sponsors and opportunities. But I have worked closely with people who have had all these advantages and still have plenty left in the tank. Why is that?

I believe it comes down to this: they don't fully bet on themselves. Betting on yourself is about knowing your values, creating a vision, expanding your influence through your network and relationships, progressing through imperfect action, and doing all these things in order to have a genuine and positive impact on the outside world. Leadership starts within you and extends outside you.

But as much as I'm a sucker for personal development, my pragmatic Dutch side is not satisfied unless there's some tangible outcome. You might be the most self-aware, balanced leader in the world, but are you putting this asset to wider use, or are you hiding your impact within your office, department or organization? The best equipment turns rusty when it's idle. Leadership is about action and service in the larger world. The true hallmark of leadership is evident when you are able to use your skills, experience and insight to create deep, positive change in a far-reaching way.

For example, when the 2008 global financial crisis hit, Finance Minister Jim Flaherty invited me and a few others to advise on key initiatives the Government of Canada could undertake to stimulate the economy. Our recommendations—a home improvement tax credit and investments in infrastructure—stimulated job creation and made a tangible difference in the lives of many Canadians. I say this with humility: the finance minister was fortunate to have a panel of seasoned business leaders, including Jim Irving from the Irving family, Jack Mintz, chair of the School of Public Policy at the University of Calgary, financier Paul Desmarais and Carole Taylor, a journalist and former B.C. minister of finance, advising him. And it was a privilege to be able to help my country in a time of need.

The more I evolve as a leader, the more I settle into my skin. I find that I'm as open-minded and willing to debate and question as ever. But experience and years of training myself to trust in and bet on me have filled me with a deep sense of confidence and knowing . . . and this knowing extends my impact even more.

There's a downside to leadership and power, however. They can corrupt. You can become so accustomed to others doing what you say and supporting your opinions that you develop a larger-than-life ego. I have seen this happen countless times, and I'm willing to bet you have as well.

There is an antidote to ego-inflation, however. The antidote to ego is purpose. *Why* do you want to lead? In the beginning, leadership is often about getting promoted and earning more money. But the "more, more" mentality leads in only one direction—egotism. Ultimately, you need to step back and examine why the privilege of leadership should be *yours* and what you'll do with the power it brings.

My purpose is quite simple: to unite sustainability and profitability and to pursue the triple bottom line where profits, people and the environment matter equally. I'm here to prove that you can run a highly profitable business that also generates excellent profits. I call it the "new capitalism." And I'm using the last stage of my career to create a company that role models new capitalism to the world. My purpose is to use all the influencing skills and power I have accumulated over the last forty years to advocate for this new way of doing business.

## THE ONE THING

As you know, I favour brilliant execution versus overwrought, fancy plans. I like to focus on the few behaviours that, if consistently executed, will produce the best results. When it comes to the new capitalism, that single behaviour is this: Take the longer view. If, as leaders we consistently challenge ourselves to consider the long-term implications of our actions, rather than immediately pursue short-term results, we will succeed in uniting profitability with sustainability.

I chair the risk committee for Liberty Mutual, an insurance company. The company invests over the long term, it quietly and carefully builds the business in new markets, and stands behind its operations in new countries, giving the business a chance to grow. They make tough decisions but this long-term strategy preserves jobs, builds long-term equity and allows the company to be more sustainable and responsible. It's a good way of doing business.

This book was born out of my twelve-month trip around the world. Stan and I travelled to dozens of countries, and everywhere we went, I saw recurring themes: environmental degradation, food and clean water scarcity, and the need for affordable, clean energy. We took a lot of pictures and many of them hang on the walls of our log house in Cape Breton—our refuge. They're beautiful photographs (when I say "we" took them, I really mean Stan took them). A former creative director, he has the eye of a true artist. But I don't hang those photographs simply because they are beautiful. I hang them because they remind me that the world is in trouble, and we have to act.

For centuries, we operated with a model of advancement that equated bigger to better, where the bottom line was the only thing that mattered, and where the growth of one thing had to mean the death of something else. That model of advancement has resulted in the troubled, beautiful world Stan and I witnessed on our adventure.

I see a new capitalism, a new model of growth and advancement that pursues the triple bottom line—people, profits and community—in equal measure. This is a model of growth that leaves the world in better shape than we found it. There are lots of business strategies that can fuel this model of advancement. For instance, implementing full-cost accounting—a model of accounting that includes the true costs of externalities—would be a useful practice. My focus in this book, however, was not on business strategies, but on people strategies. And not on many strategies, but on one in particular: the strategy of being yourself and letting your true humanity shine through.

More than four decades in business has convinced me that, despite the very real existence of "alligators" and hidden agendas, most people are genuinely good. And if we can get clear on our values, and develop the courage to lead with them, we will naturally pursue a model of growth and advancement that is good for the world.

When I was at Home Depot, a receiving manager approached me one day while I was walking a store. "Annette, look at what we're throwing away," he said. He led me to a section of a storeroom that held a number of kitchen cabinets that had sustained some minor damage during shipping—we couldn't sell them, but they were still perfectly serviceable. "There are so many people who could use these cabinets, people who could not afford to come into our store to buy them new." I was on the board of Habitat for Humanity and told them about the situation. One of my colleagues tabled the idea of re-stores, which would sell cabinets and other home products at heavily discounted prices to people who really needed them. At first, I met a lot of resistance within Home Depot. It's not that people didn't want to help; they just didn't see how we could do so without undercutting our existing business. Why would someone come into the store to buy a perfect cabinet when they could buy a similar version for half the price down the road? Our suppliers would be up in arms, they said. But together, we worked out a way to stamp the product and thereby ensure it could be sold only at designated stores reserved for low-income homeowners, and could not come back "into the system" and be sold at stores that competed with Home Depot. We were providing useful items to people in need at a highly reduced price, diverting products from the landfill, and recouping some investment on the inventory that we would have otherwise lost. Any way you cut it, it was a good thing. That's new capitalism in action.

Capitalism is a force for good, I truly believe this. But to marry the pursuit of profit with a longer-term view that combines altruism with pragmatism—this takes guts. You have to disrupt the status quo and, yet again, bet on *you*.

I wanted to reduce energy consumption in Home Depot's Canadian stores. Together, the team devised a strategy that would see fifty percent of a store's lights go out when the outdoor temperatures rose above 30 degrees Celsius. The U.S. CEO thought it was going too far, and argued with me that he "couldn't see his way through the store," while we were doing a walk-through. I stood my ground. "Your eyes are adjusting, it's normal," I said. Despite pressure to discard our strategy, we stuck to the plan and we reduced energy costs by thirteen percent in our stores, and even grew sales during this period. This kind of initiative—the decision to risk making some people unhappy in order to do the right thing—is what will advance our world from a model of growth that puts profit above everything else, to a model of true, long-term advancement that values profit, people and the environment.

I have worked beside, mentored and sponsored hundreds of people. Time and again, I have witnessed how a willingness to drop the games and truly embrace the people we are enhances communication, improves team performance and brings out the integrity of individuals, teams and companies as a whole.

I hope this book and my personal story have inspired you to feel comfortable in your skin and lead as the person you are. The more we're able to do this, the better our world will be.

# ACKNOWLEDGEMENTS

Everything I have accomplished (and I mean everything) has been the result of a team effort, including this book. Stanislaus Shibinsky (Stan), my husband, tops this list for so patiently supporting me in writing this book as I lead a start-up as well as invest my time in for-profit and non-profit board work. I love you to the stars and back.

A big shout-out to my Canadian and Netherlands family: Your unending practical and emotional support has been the true constant of my life. Your love, cajoling and empathy have kept me grounded and inspired during the highs and lows of a fully lived life. Special thanks to my sister, Dorothy, for encouraging me to start this project.

To my colleagues and friends, past and present: The stories, wisdom and practical advice I share here are the culmination of almost four decades working with and learning from some of the most brilliant and caring people on the planet. Thank you for your faith and trust. Thank you especially to Eleanor Beaton from Nova Scotia and Jim Gifford from HarperCollins for working with me to tell my story.

To my teachers and mentors: Theresa Musgrave, Gwen Sheperd, Margie McCain, Mary Susanne Lamont (and the ladies of the lake), Liz Parr-Johnston, Bea Crawford, Her Excellency Sharon Johnston, Lorraine Mitchelmore, Zita Cobb, Elyse Allen, Sarita Mandanna, Linda Hasenfratz, Dr. Cindy Wahler, Amanda Lang, Ilse Treurnicht, the late Mona Campbell, Wendy Evans, Catherine Zahn, Andrea Rosen, Arlene Dickenson, Carol Tomé, Darrell Gregersen, Dr. Janet Smith, Anne Patterson, Ellen Rudnick, Myrtle Porter, Marian Heard, Madeleine Paquin, Annalisa King, Catherine Best, Joy Romero, Allison Blunt, Larysa Osmak, Erblin Rexha and Cathy Morra—strong, determined women who inspired me to lead.

Thanks also to David Miller (Antigonish), Steve Rankin, George Currie, D'Arcy McKeough, Keith Eldridge, Joe Shannon, Jack Bush, Brian McDonnell, Jerry Payton, Arthur Blank and Bernie Marcus, Bill Lennie, Bob Nardelli, Frank Blake, Dominic Barton, John Manley, David Patterson, Frank McKenna, Jim Irving, Ted Kelly, David Long, Calin Rovinescu, Lino Saputo, Jr., Murray Edwards, Lou Serafini, Jr., Joe Cofelice, Paul Desmarais, Jr., Tom D'Aquino, John Bragg, the late Irving Schwartz, David and Donald Sobey, John Risley, Michael McCain, John Harker, Ross McCurdy, David Wheeler and so many of my east coast sponsors, and the smart and caring Governor General David Johnston. And I owe a great debt of gratitude to a great man, the late Purdy Crawford, for betting on me countless times. Without your support, I would not have had the career I have had.

To the next generation of leaders: The hope and inspiration I feel when I work with emerging leaders is truly what inspired and motivated me to start this project. Mentorship and sponsorship is a powerful force for growth and development; I wrote this book as a way to offer what I have learned in business and in life to many more people than I possibly can reach face to face. Take this book, learn from it, be entertained by it and know that my sincere hope is that my words will empower you to step up, have courage and bet on yourself.

To my mighty team at NRStor: Jason, Jen, Alexander, Katherine, Geoff, Shivani, Allison and Colton, thank you for what we are building together—I have one career left in me, and this could be the one that gives us all the most pride. We make money and give back to our world. It doesn't get any better than this.